An Uncommon Task

& Other Stories
Carle O'Neil

Editor: Elizabeth Watts
Publications Director: Patricia L. Millard
Cover design and illustration: Ralph Butler

ISBN 0-929310-19-5

Printed in the U.S.A. by St. Mary's Press, Washington, D.C.

Contents

Publisher's Foreword

There are many stories to be told in corrections. Unfortunately, the vast majority that are told deal with crowding, escapes, riots, and recidivism. Rarely does the public hear about the more common, everyday things that happen in corrections: the former "juvenile delinquent" who makes good; the positive relationships between inmates and staff members that really make a difference; the laughter and tears that are also part of the corrections experience.

We at the American Correctional Association are pleased to publish this collection of short stories by my former colleague Carle O'Neil that deal with the human, personal side of corrections. Carle has worked in almost every aspect of corrections–juvenile probation, adult parole, juvenile detention, and adult institutions for men and women. His breadth of experience and depth of feeling show in these stories. Members of the general public and correctional practitioners alike will gain a more balanced, humanistic view of the field through this fine collection.

The ACA is always interested in publishing your thoughts. Maybe Carle's work will inspire you.

Anthony P. Travisono
Executive Director

Foreword

We human beings are unhappy and lonely in isolation. We need the company of other humans to appreciate and share our human condition. We rarely feel better than when another person lets us know that we are understood and appreciated. Isolation may be caused by distance, by walls or fences, or by barriers of language, race, class, or sex; and just as effectively by a lack of understanding.

We are at our best as human beings when we appreciate and accept other human beings; not gullibly, but with true understanding and tolerance. In this way we grow in our humanity. We progress as human beings as we become more able to share the human experience with more of humankind. The man who cannot understand the feelings of women is limited as a human being. The teacher who cannot understand the feelings of children will not be a good teacher. The judge who cannot understand the feelings of the prisoner at the bar should not be a judge.

Boys and girls and men and women in our criminal justice system are especially likely to be the victims of social rejection, hostility, and isolation. Indeed, there is no group so widely and so severely excluded from understanding and acceptance in human society as those convicted of violating the criminal law. This is not to disparage the need for law and a system of justice. Rather, it is an expression of regret that the possibilities of encouraging lawful behavior through simple human understanding are so widely neglected.

Carle O'Neil was the superintendent of a training school for delinquent boys when he recruited me to work there. He guided me in that work, and we learned much together. Now, from a varied career in the field of corrections, he brings us a collection of stories that speak with authority. Carle O'Neil understands what he is writing about.

The reader may well be surprised to find that the distance between him or herself and some of the principal characters of these stories—

clients of the criminal justice system—has been reduced. He or she may indeed feel an identification with the essential humanity of those characters even though they have offended against the social order.

Besides being interesting, this book may be useful in advancing the reader's understanding of the inmate of whom I wrote privately years ago:

> The deadly dull monotony of endless day on day,
> The grim relentless monody, unending day on day,
> The prison air, the prison fare, the prison suits of gray,
> The deadly dull monotony of endless day on day.
> The bucket walk, the whispered talk, the rats that they'll repay!
> The prison yards, the prison guards, the life that's shut away,
> The deadly dull monotony of endless day on day,
> It soaks into the convict's brain and eats his mind away.

Richard L. Jenkins, M.D.
Professor of Child Psychiatry (Emeritus)
University of Iowa College of Medicine

Introduction

By pleasant coincidence, I recently resumed contact with a former associate of whom I had lost sight for thirty-five years. Over lunch, we sketched for one another high points of our careers. As I told of having spent the time working in prisons and juvenile training schools, I was briefly shocked to hear my friend say, "Why would a man like you ever have wanted to spend his life with those awful people, those criminals and delinquents?" With a shrug and a smile I dodged the question; it was one that had been put to me before, but never by a "liberal" who had devoted many years to active politics on behalf of organized labor, good schools, and the teaching profession. Her attitude toward prisons and inmates was typical of many, insofar as they think of prisons at all.

Prisons and corrections do not stand very high on the public interest scale. Some people have a vague curiosity about what prisons are like and what goes on in them; others are inclined to regard penitentiaries as necessary but not noteworthy. They are places to which wrongdoers are banished, generally for too short a time, under conditions that should be sufficiently severe to make them regret their criminality, to incapacitate them from further depredating the open community for at least the duration of their sentences, and, it is hoped, to scare them into behaving better after their release—if they must be released.

Simultaneously, however, a majority of the public vaguely holds, without strongly advocating, that during imprisonment something should be done in the way of "education" or "counseling" or some other kind of "intervention" that will so alter the lives of inmates that they will emerge as less predatory and more acceptable human beings.

Since there must be prisons, there must be someone in charge of them, maintaining order and directing their day-to-day activities. But just why anyone would deliberately choose such an occupation is difficult to say.

It seems safe to say that generally one does not choose corrections to make a fortune (although fortunes have been made in such work) or to achieve power (although political power has accrued to some prison officials). The corrections worker does not stand high on the social status ladder. This is not surprising in a culture where human service professions are not customarily highly regarded occupations. Teaching, for instance, while acknowledged to be of real importance for the success of democracy and for the fulfillment of individual lives, is not much honored, rewarded, or revered. Further down the scale are social workers or correctional employees, who may receive the occasional indulgence of an invitation to speak before a service club, but who for the most part are out of sight and out of mind.

So why then, to return to my friend's question, would one choose to spend a lifetime working with criminals and delinquents? The answer is much more complicated than the question, for while one may consciously choose to follow a given line of work, the choice is likely predicated on factors of one's character, along with influences on one's upbringing and education, plus the element of happenstance or luck.

My inherent nature was such that I developed an interest in and was eager to know about those people whose behaviors landed them in the courts and institutions. More than making money or achieving high social status or political power, I wanted to know what made such individuals tick and how they could be changed–corrected. As opportunities to follow up these interests came along, I took them where another with a different bent might not even have seem them.

My earliest recollection of "imprisonment" dates to when I was a fourth grader. One morning, as we were on our way to school, a companion said to me, "Did you know that Jasper and Turner were sent away to reform school yesterday?" I knew Jasper and Turner. Since I lived closer to the right side of town than they did, I had often been a target for their threats, taunts, and snowballs. They were big, tough kids, and I was afraid of them.

I was not clear about what a reform school was, however. My companion didn't know much about it either, except that it was a place where bad kids were sent to be locked up and otherwise punished. Whatever it was, I was glad that these two had been sent there; I hoped that they would be there for a long time. Until years later, when I finally visited one, I had a lingering curiosity about what a training school was like.

As far as my choice to work in corrections was a conscious one, it was abetted by the influence that my early training, especially a Christian upbringing, had on me. I was started in Sunday school with the cradle roll and continued through high school. More than once my mother told me that she hoped I might become a minister. That did not appeal to me, but I did believe the teachings of Jesus to be profound truths–divine in the sense that they were inspired–offering salvation to mankind, not in an unknown hereafter, but right now in the present if we could incorporate them into our daily lives.

Another very important influence came from school, with the fortunate guidance of some outstanding teachers. There, among much else, I learned of the practical, historical translation of the fundamental principles of Christianity (but common to all great religions) into the legal concepts of justice, freedom, and social responsibility that were written into our Constitution.

From these two influences, religious and secular, my convictions were firmly molded: that one has a responsibility to his or her fellow man, that an important element of being human is to care for and assist other human beings, and that fairness or justice is a fragile underpinning of human survival requiring constant husbandry.

As a boy and young adult, the thought of working with delinquents or criminals had never occurred to me as a vocation for which to plan and prepare. I stumbled into the work.

Following World War II, as an elected member of the legislature of my state, I visited a number of public institutions, including a prison and two training schools, with other members of the legislative appropriations committee. One of the training schools visited was that to which my tormentors had been sent when I was a fourth grader. Its physical plant was dismal, but I was impressed with a number of the staff members, who described the situations from which their charges came and how they attempted to deal with them in a reformative way. The state prison presented an even more stunning experience. Its walls were grim; the interior was stark and fearsome. Its inmates were not the cleanly scrubbed, often wistfully appealing kids at the training schools but more often frowning, threatening, unknowns staring out from steel cages.

In spite of the pervasive sense of malice and mistrust, I felt a great curiosity to know more about the place. What really goes on in here? More important, what really goes on in the heads of these inmates? What combination of factors brought them here? What combination of factors could bring changes in them that would "safen" them up and contribute to their acceptability in their remaining days? I remembered that a family friend had once been sent to the prison for theft of mail. He had never been an evil, threatening person. After two years in prison he had returned to his home and family and lived out the rest of his life respectably. How many of these staring faces were such as he? Someday, I thought vaguely, I am going to get involved in finding answers to these questions. The opportunity came sooner that I had expected.

Not long after the close of the legislative session (I had come to the realization that the public spotlight and a political career were not for me), a chance arose to take a job as a juvenile probation officer. I took it, leaving my father's business and going to work for a district court judge at half the pay. I spent my first three years in corrections as the only probation officer for two geographically large but thinly populated counties in Montana. I was fortunate to work for a judge who took his responsibility for juvenile court seriously, although it was only a part of his workload. I learned a lot about devotion to principles, forthrightness, unpretentious decency, and moral courage from that country judge.

After three years I went back to graduate school, where I expected to find answers to some of the questions confronting me. Graduate school was a broadening experience, painful in some ways, but it did not give me the answers about the causes and remedies for delinquent behavior that I had naively assumed that someone "out there" must have.

I completed graduate school, and after two years of adult parole service in Oakland, I transferred inside the walls of the California state prison at San Quentin as a member of an experimental intensive treatment unit.

The intensive treatment unit was a unique and potentially invaluable experiment. It consisted of seven social workers, two psychologists, and a part-time psychiatrist and had been in existence for over two years when I arrived. Each of the therapists had a caseload of fifteen to twenty-five inmates with whom they met for up to five times a week in individual and group sessions. The principal intent of the program was to demonstrate that intensive counseling/psychotherapy would result in improved behavior when the recipient inmates returned to the open community. The experimental subjects were selected at random from a pool of inmates who met certain selection criteria; after their release from prison their records were to be compared with those of a control group of inmates who had not been involved in the intensive counseling.

Almost from its inception, the intensive treatment unit had become a focal point of the rivalrous custody/treatment dichotomy so prevalent in many correctional institutions. Every few weeks, one could count on arriving for work at unit headquarters to find that they had been ransacked. Unannounced searches for contraband at locations throughout the prison were required and justified by the nature of the place, but in no location were they conducted with the vandalistic flair awarded the intensive treatment unit, a rueful illustration of the egregious, pervasive rivalry among prison employees of divergent points of professional view.

I had been with the intensive treatment unit for about three years when it was abruptly discontinued for "budgetary considerations." Economy was a factor, but the program had made itself convenient for cost-saving sacrifice by the shockingly poor performance of its highly educated staff. While they shared a common goal, they were sadly rivalrous among themselves and almost obsessive in their vociferous criticism of the prison administration.

After several years in adult prisons, including a year at the California Institution for Women, I returned to work with juveniles as a member of the executive staff of the Iowa Training School for Boys at a rare time when the essentials of gifted leadership and public and political support were ripe for change. Traditional departments of custody and treatment were combined under one administrative head. Employees were no longer able to cling to rivalrous sides. There was only one side, and that was teamwork on behalf of the residents.

I am pleased to have had a significant role in this institutional transition. The things that I seriously and consciously believe in, whether stated in religious terms such as the Sermon on the Mount or in legalistic terms such as responsibility and justice, were our unequivocal objectives. With my own eyes I saw and with my own hands I contributed to the accomplishment of a noble endeavor.

Throughout my working years I was intrigued by prisons and training schools; by a need to know about the residents of such places, encouraged—or perhaps compelled—by the philosophical belief that these individuals required humanitarian but realistic service. I had a constantly regenerating ambition to learn about the roots of delinquency and criminal behavior in the hope that appropriate corrective measures might be understood and applied for the protection of society, the alleviation of human suffering, and the more acceptable fulfillment of human lives.

The stories that follow arise from incidents along the way in this career. Each of them is a combination of fact and fiction. Generally, the more difficult a story may be to believe, the more factual is its content.

You Goes Home At Night

Tuesday morning. I checked in through the sally port a few minutes late as sometimes happened. The two officers were courteous without sacrificing a professional reserve. No one ever bothered me about my occasional tardiness. I was always there for an hour or two—sometimes more—after quitting time, which more than made up for slow starts. The staff gossips in their hushed corners ridiculed me, I knew, for my long days; to them, spending extra time on a job like mine was misguided at best.

As I walked the length of the administration building and turned into the special services wing, I was greeted pleasantly by most of the inmates, who were on their way to work assignments or sick call. From a few there were coldly hostile stares; and from one or two, there were shameless, smiling come-ons, partly because I have some power in this place, but also because I'm male and in good shape. "Baby, what I wants is a man!" I heard someone say behind me.

Bright sunshine streaming through my office window highlighted the fresh yellow roses in a vase on the oak desk. Just how the cleaning woman got flowers into my locked office before my arrival each day was one of several mysteries that I had never bothered to solve. After five months of working in this prison of 850 women inmates, I had learned to accept a few such special attentions.

Still, I frequently marvel at how loose the place is in some ways. No prison for men could operate for very long with as few custodians as this one does. For instance, inmates are not supposed to enter the administration building without a pass, but they frequently do. There just are not enough supervisors to closely watch the two entrances from the prison yard. To help the staff maintain control there is an odd, acknowledged, but unwritten, reliance on the docility and desire for peace and safety of most of the inmates. The relatively few real troublemakers are clearly known. Their potential for tantrums, even attack, is quietly balanced by others who are strategically assigned in the certainty that they–the "staff-minded"–will come to the aid of staff in the event of a rumble. Problems, sometimes of almost desperate intensity, do arise, and they are generally met by female line staff with a quiet, unyielding resignation quite unlike the macho, frontal force observed in an institution for males.

My appointment calendar, I saw, represented a jumble of human troubles to be dealt with during the morning. In the afternoon, two and a half hours were blocked out for the weekly Classification Committee meeting. I was not quite ready to take up any of it yet, and so I turned my back on the calendar and drifted over to look out the window, prolonging the start of the day.

The prison campus is a remarkably attractive setting if you ignore the high, viciously sharp security fence posted far out around the rambling, single-story, Spanish-style cottages. Many a small-college board of trustees might be delighted to have the neat, green lawns, the weedless, rich flower beds, and the carefully pruned trees of this human eddy. Here and there I saw inmates, singly and in pairs, working in the gardens, trimming grass, hoeing. For a mindless moment I envied them their work in the sunshine. As I recognized faces I made barely conscious review of their names and, in some cases, their crimes and the sentences they were serving.

Some distance out I saw Mandy Washington and her friend Constance–I could not recall her last name—walking hand-in-hand. As relaxed and cheerful as they seemed to be, they could have been on a stroll through Golden Gate Park. Halfway in from the greenhouse they stopped and sat down casually on the grass, pulling their cotton skirts tightly around their folded legs. With hand shears they snipped at a few blades of grass, but mostly they were engrossed in conversation, oblivious of anything around them.

Mandy is well-known here. That is not because she is always pleasant. And she is not one to hide her mood or her demands under any kind of a false front. If there is something she wants she goes after it, sometimes by guile, but more often with taut-faced, vocal aggression, backed up by lean, almost masculine, muscles.

I remembered my first encounter with her months before, shortly after I had been transferred here as an experimental male on the all-female executive staff. She had, indeed, made quite an impression on me. I had been late to work that morning too, and as I had walked along the corridor a willowy young woman stepped out from behind a doorway, confronting me with the choice of stopping or of forcing my way past her. Her vaguely oriental eyes were angry, threatening.

"I want to talk wit'choo, man," she said through even, white teeth in a tone of voice that did not promise me a presentation of man-of-the-year award. Her right hand rested on a pair of grass shears tucked beneath the sash of her dress.

Although the confrontation had caught me by surprise and probably raised my blood pressure, it seemed to be a time for calm control rather than a heated response. I was larger than my accoster and, as I said before, I stay in good shape. Were she to physically attack me I was confident that I could handle her even if she pulled the shears. I was cautious and at the same time puzzled.

"You and I can talk," I said, "but this is not the time or the place. If you will tell me who you are, I will see you in my office when I can arrange it. I am not going to put you ahead of others who already have appointments just because you have pushed your way in here without a pass. It's my job to see you when I can, and I will."

Mandy showed a flicker of disbelief; it seemed a surprise to her that I did not know her name, prideful as she was of a certain notoriety. She was checking me out. Could she intimidate this new, questionable addition to the staff? She told me her name, all the while maintaining a menacing demeanor.

"Go back to your work detail now. I will send for you when I have an opening. Then we'll talk."

Mandy lowered her arms and took half a step to one side—enough to let me pass by, but not enough to be called capitulation.

"I'll go back outside, man, but don't mess up on callin' me, hear!"

Some people, I suppose, would wag their heads and call me another mollycoddling do-gooder, ridiculing me for my restrained response. I'll admit that a resort to angry force in the face of such an aggressive attitude is a fairly natural and tempting way to react, but that does not make it appropriate. Sometimes, from the vestibule of one's consciousness comes a cue to make the proper move. I had recognized Mandy's action as a threat, but it was short of an attack. Hers was a primitive effort to get what she wanted from me and to put me on notice for the future. She had been surviving in her ghetto existence for a lifetime by force and intimidation. My job is not to play her game, but to conduct a live demonstration of alternatives to ghetto games whenever possible. Rightly, prison is supposed to take offenders out of the free community, but it should do more than just "salt them away"; if possible, it should teach them something. Too often prison teaches little that is worthwhile for the inmate or, in the long run, for society because there isn't the know-how or the manpower or the inclination to do so.

Later, I had met with Mandy Washington as promised, and I had listened to a rather generalized string of complaints about the injustice of her imprisonment, the poor quality of the food, and the stupidity of the staff. More specifically, she said that the one good thing in here is her friendship with a girl with whom she works on the grounds crew; however, if you have a close friend in this place you get hassled, for it is at once assumed by many that you are "queer." Mandy and her friend were doubly suspect and disapproved of because Mandy has a very dark complexion and her friend is a very fair. So they constantly "got it" from those who couldn't stand interracial relationships as well as those who saw overt sexuality in almost every close friendship. This, she said, is a sample of staff stupidity. Nobody had ever caught her and her friend at "nothin' other than conversation and never would." She'd told the warden about it, she said, and now she was tellin' me about it, and we ought to do somethin' about it! It had become clear to me that she was an intelligent, vocal person with an enormous reservoir of primitive aggression, one who could be a willful and uncompromising handful.

Seeing Mandy out there now on the grass with her friend reminded me that she was on the schedule for this afternoon's Classification Committee meeting. That could mean an active session! The beautiful weather had given me a touch of spring fever, and I'd prefer easier going this afternoon.

The Classification Committee meets each Tuesday afternoon in the pleasant, mahogany-paneled conference room of the attractive administration building. It is the committee's purpose to assign inmates to their living quarters, workplaces, and studies. To chair the meetings of the five-member group is one of my duties.

While the personal potentials and programs of inmates interest me, and I regard their placements very seriously, the pressure of the number to be seen in the time available generally does not allow for very sensitive, individualized attention. It can be an emotional occasion for inmates, who often have strong hopes for certain placements. The committee must hastily determine the major elements of their prison existence. In the sense that the Lord giveth and the Lord taketh away, the prison Classification Committee is God.

Three of the committee members are executively powerful, late-middle-aged department heads who don't do much to make life cheery. Much like inmates they are "doing time," awaiting longed-for retirement. What human warmth they may once have had has long since burned out, leaving them opinionated and heedless. In fairness, it must be acknowledged that, over the years, they have had to manage the lives of hundreds of difficult personalities with frightfully meager help. Still, I have little patience with their decay. I recognize that I am no more popular with them than they are with me: I am a brash newcomer to be endured, hardly welcomed, barely tolerated–a healthy male whose presence, they are convinced, will inevitably result in scandal.

Brent Sanders, the fifth member of the committee, is a senior counselor, a position that does not entail administrative responsibility; this leaves him at the bottom of the formal power ladder. And, being severely crippled by arthritis, he is no physical (sexual) threat to anyone; he is ambulatory only with the greatest, most deliberate effort. But in that inflamed body is a bright mind and buoyant good will. Though in constant physical pain, he has not lost the ability to care about social misfits, most of whom he genuinely regards as less fortunate than himself. He also has a bubbling sense of humor, and his wit often lightens the oppressive atmosphere and breaks the logjam of emotional situations.

The conference room was very warm on this early summer afternoon in spite of a large electric fan that stood whirring on its shiny steel pedestal. As the meeting commenced, two of the three women were atypically jocular; they were pushing congeniality a little obviously today. Mrs. Sigmont, director of education, condescended me a smile. "Are you ready for the full agenda, Mr. Rosen?" she asked with a wicked-witch cackle, her fleshy arms jiggling. I got her message: Mandy Washington's name was one of twelve on the agenda and Sigmont was dreading the encounter.

The first to be seen, however, was a newly arrived inmate who had not been to classification before. Susan Bricker was a former secretary who, with her boss/doctor/lover, had killed his wife and who was now at the entry level of a life sentence. She was startlingly attractive, with light, clear skin and a look of youthful vulnerability that I had trouble reconciling with all of the stories about her that had been carried in the papers during the extended trial. As she entered the room, then sat before us, there was no hint in her manner or appearance of a capacity for premeditated murder. The women of the committee regarded her in a distant way. They had seen many murderers over the years, although few whose cases were so notorious as this one.

Inmate Bricker requested an opportunity to work out of doors, and she was quickly assigned to the gardening crew. Come winter, she would probably seek a change, but that was all right; she would be here long enough to make several changes. The interview was short with few questions asked and no demands made. As Bricker left the room Sigmont sneered, "She's been here six weeks and I understand that she's already got a 'friend!'"

Brent Sanders gave me a raised-brow, rolled-eyeballs comment without otherwise moving his head.

The second girl–the older staff members call all of the inmates "girls"–wasn't going to trouble anyone. She was a poor, dumb creature with sleepy eyes and big lips that hung open. Her accumulated rage at an indolent mate had been expressed by mayhem: she had poured scalding water over him as he lay asleep in bed. The man had survived, but he had been horribly scarred. The woman seemed frightened and confused, making little sense except when she asked if she would be able to have visits from her kids. She was quickly assigned to the laundry, where she could work away the months and be forgotten. No one else picked up on the creature's question, so I told her that visits with children were to be encouraged and that we would do what we could to arrange them. I made a note to follow up. We would have to find out where the children were living; then, a volunteer in the community would need to be found to bring them to the prison during visiting hours. To work out the details might take some time. Making such arrangements was what kept me working late many nights.

Next on the list was the name of Mandy Washington–today's unsolicited challenge. Before she was called the ladies became subdued, their faces solemn behind Kabuki-like masks of powder and rouge. As with the other cases, Brent Sanders gave a summary of pertinent information, stiffly sorting through his notes with knotted fingers. His spine was rigidly arched, so that he leaned over the table like a bamboo fishing pole, his face not far above a stack of manila folders. From a number of conversations with Mandy he had developed a respect, even a fondness, for her that put him a class by himself so far as the staff was concerned. With a detachment enforced by his disease, he was amused by her success at upsetting people. Her perversity, he saw, had been a main means of survival in the West Oakland ghetto where she had grown up.

"I guess you all know," Brent said through rigid jaws and with a chuckle hoarse from constant doses of aspirin, "Mandy has been here for fourteen months of a ten-year sentence. She carried the gun while a male accomplice scooped $200 from the till of an L.A. liquor store. The guy, by the way, has never been caught. She hasn't had much schooling, but I'd say she's one of the brighter inmates here. She likes her work on the lawn crew, and that is a good outlet for her physical energy. She loves flowers and is very particular about how the lawns are kept. Mandy has a friend on the grounds detail, Constance Mahew. They spend a lot of time together."

Brent added that Constance, a pretty woman of gentle nature, poetic and shy, had been convicted on a series of drug charges. "'Mandy has taken Constance under her wing and they are pretty close. Mandy is asking to be transferred from Homestead Cottage to Collins Hall where Constance lives."

The ladies stared at the table, not looking at Brent as he spoke. When he finished they had no questions. I leaned on the arm of my upholstered chair wondering more about how Brent, so severely crippled, makes it through a day than about Mandy's history.

When summoned from the waiting area, Mandy entered the room smiling uncharacteristically, like graduation day at Dale Carnegie's, and sat down in the red leather chair at the end of the long, gleaming, conference table. My female colleagues responded with nods, and in their glance there seemed to be the hope that Mandy would be nice today; maybe they could connive their way through this. Brent's and Mandy's eyes flickered a greeting with warmth from him and an acknowledgement of his presence from her. She avoided looking at me. She was wearing a prison-issue, cotton-print work dress tied tightly around her slender waist with a knee-length sash of some faded material. Tucked under the sash on her right side were her grass shears. It was a little odd that the work supervisor had let Mandy come to this meeting carrying the shears. But, as I said before, things are oddly loose around here in some ways.

Sigmont shifted her matronly bulk in her leather chair and, with phony warmth, said, "How are you today, Mandy?"

It was such a honeyed greeting that Brent Sanders looked away, and I bit my lip in embarrassment. Mandy's own I'll-charm-the-hell-out-of-you smile flattened to a look of caution. Nobody was going to sweet-talk her, but she answered, "Fine," in a civil tone.

Sigmont did not miss Mandy's wariness and hurried on to her idea of business. "Mandy, you are here this afternoon because you have requested a change from your present dormitory to Collins Hall. Is that correct?"

"Tha's right," said Mandy, swaying slightly.

"Is there something you are unhappy with in your present cottage?" Sigmont was a trifle too sweet again.

Tentatively looking at Sigmont as though she'd got a whiff of something bad-smelling, Mandy said "No, Homestead Cottage is a nice place. The girls there gets along all right and the staffs is all nice. They all nice. I just wants to be over in Collins."

"Are you trying to get away from some trouble in Homestead? Are you in debt to somebody there? Is somebody putting pressure on you?" asked Sigmont.

"No, Miss Sigmont. They ain't nobody in here puts pressure on me for nothin'!" A threatening edge had come into Mandy's voice; she glanced at me for the first time since entering the room. Sigmont withdrew, suddenly becoming engrossed in creating a ballpoint sketch on her yellow note pad.

Director of Custody Emma Bingham leaned forward on her chair, her tiny feet in shiny black pumps swinging just off of the floor as she took up the role of principal interrogator. "Mother Big-ham," the inmates call her among themselves, with derision. She was sharp-featured, impeccably made-up, wearing a silk dress printed with bright, blotchy flowers.

"You are just asking for a change in cottages and no change in your work detail, is that correct?" At least Bingham was not honeyed. With the fingers of her left hand she drummed the table, several diamond rings catching the light impressively.

"Correct," replied Mandy. Hostility had displaced condescension in her eyes; the black skin over her high cheekbones was shining with perspiration.

"And you say that this is not because of any troubles that you may be having in the cottage?" Bingham was being cunningly obtuse.

"No, Miss Big . . . uh . . . Bingham. They ain't no trouble in the cottage; if they was I'm sure you would have knowed it without askin' me. I would jes like to live in Collins, and I'm askin' to be assigned there." Mandy was making a clutching effort at reasonability.

"Your friend Constance lives in Collins Hall doesn't she, Mandy?" Bingham's lips formed a half-smile, but her eyes were coldly questioning–accusing–over the tops of her rimless glasses. The barbed-wire lady, dressed like she was going to church, was playing a cat-and-mouse game. She could have been a Nazi.

Sigmont, rejoining the proceedings, pursed her lips and, with half-closed eyelids, looked past Mandy into some vast source of mystical enlightenment and said, "Mandy, you are asking for a transfer of cottages so you can be close to a friend?"

Oh, Jesus, I thought. Here it comes.

"Yes, ma'am. Tha's what I'm askin'. I wants to live by her. I'd ask to be assigned roommates, but I know you couldn't stand that. If we lives in the same cottage we can spend our spare time together." Mandy's anger was still controlled, but her chest thrust forward, her right fist was clenched, showing ashy knuckles.

Mrs. Wiedenbacker, records officer, sat with stubby fingers clasped in her lap, looking from Mandy to Bingham to Sigmont through thick, owl-eyed lenses. She abhorred inmates, wanted nothing to do with them. Emotional confrontations were apt to give her sick headaches. She usually said nothing in these meetings unless it was to call out to someone in her office for supplemental information on the telephone, which sat near her on the table. Inmates and their lives were incidental to her compulsive burden of flawless recordkeeping.

In sing-song sarcasm, Bingham said, "You and Constance work together in the yard and now you want to live together in the same cottage?" She'd been watching the growing friendship between these two for some time and had firmly concluded that it meant just one disgusting thing.

"Right," said Mandy with an electric stare, fully perceptive of "Bigham's" opinion.

Brent Sanders, with his irrepressible good will, said, "Mandy, you and Constance are very different in a lot of ways, but you are friends."

Good old Brent, I thought, setting himself up as Mandy's straight man. Over the weeks Mandy had come to accord Brent something as close to respect as she would allow any official. She had at first disdained him as a cripple, but her code excluded kicking an underdog, even a white one, and she had come to recognize his intelligence and fairness.

"Sure, we different," replied Mandy. "She white; I's black. I ain't scared of nobody. She shy and soft and could get eat up alive in this messed-up place. She needs the strength in me. In here we makes life bearable. We is two friends."

Brent nodded.

Bingham gave Brent a look of patronizing disbelief that said, "Surely, you should be able to see the truth about a pair like this."

After a heavy and prolonged silence, which added up to impasse, I asked if there were any more questions. There was no response.

To Mandy I said, "Is there anything more that you would like to say, Miss Washington?"

Mandy gave a muffled snort. With a mixture of anger and despair, but with a certain dignity, she said, "I have made a simple request to be transferred from Homestead to Collins. I wants to make that move. You people spends a lots of time here, but you goes home at night. You can't know what it is like to spend you whole life in here. Someone you can trust, a friend, is all that keeps you goin' sometimes. Most of you can't understand that or else you don't care. Me and Constance is friends. We don't hurt nobody. We needs each other. All we askin' is let us live in the same cottage."

After another silence I asked Mandy to step out of the room while the committee considered her request. Her out-thrust chin and swinging hips showed that she knew that no discussion was needed. She'd been sizing up peoples' votes all of her twenty-three years, and it was obvious to her how this ballot would go.

She was right. There was very little discussion. Minds were made up and talk would not alter them. The vote was two to allow the transfer and three to deny the request.

Mandy was called back. She stood behind the red leather chair awaiting word of the decision. Without inviting her to be seated I told her that the committee had voted not to grant her request. "You will not be permitted to transfer out of Homestead Cottage to Collins Hall."

There was an immediate human explosion. Fire came from Mandy's eyes as she crouched slightly and whirled like a discus thrower, overturning the electric fan from its pedestal to the floor, bright sparks flying as the motor mechanism broke apart, and all the time she yelled, "You dirty fuckers! Your heads are full of shit! Every friendship is dirt to you! Bastards!"

With startling strength, she raised the red leather chair shoulder high and swung it across the room, breaking off one hardwood leg as it hit the polished-panel wall. She spun back, her bare arms brushing a chrome thermos of icewater from the table, shattering it in a mess on the floor. She jerked the telephone from its cord, lifted it over her head and smashed it down in the water and the debris of the fan, pieces of white plastic and a brass bell rattling out across the red tiles. Speechless, the women eyed her.

Standing athletically erect, glaring at each of us, Mandy pulled the grass shears from the sash at her waist with a flourish, and, waving them, said, "Don't none of you fuckers come near me!"

The matrons sat like plastic bags of compost. Brent's eyes were huge in his immobile body. I was sharply aware that I was the only staff member in the room who could take action in this outburst, which I had not caused and could not prevent. Now I had the honor of single-handedly putting the lid on the action. I stood up, wishing for more mobility than I felt in a suit and tie, and moved left around the long table. As I got halfway to Mandy she turned and fled out through the heavy, carved door without another word. I followed.

The long, waxed hallway was deserted. Doorways stood open into quiet office spaces. The whole place seemed to be on siesta. How could everyone have missed the sounds of the micro-Hiroshima that had just occurred in the conference room? Why wasn't someone coming to investigate?

Mandy strode toward the corridor's far end and the untended door to the yard; she took steps as long as her skirt would allow, her lean, muscular arms swinging vigorously and her flat heels scrape-scraping across the linoleum squares. She did not look back.

I would like to say that I had a plan, but I did not. This show had to stop, but thus far Mandy was its sole producer. I saw not one person who might give a hand—no supervisor, no "staff-minded" inmate who would duck into an office and signal the officers to come from the front entrance. As it worked out, that was just as well.

Arriving at the heavy security door through which Mandy had gone to the yard, I could hear shouts and greetings from outside. I was surprised by the presence of twenty-five or thirty inmates who were congregated there. All were in cotton work frocks; some wore kerchiefs on their heads; a few leaned on rakes and hoes. It seemed as if half of the grounds detail had been awaiting Mandy's return. I had felt confident that I could deal with Mandy alone if I had to, but I was uneasy about this unexpected group of sympathizers. Would they be stirred to a biting, kicking, rioting ruckus?

As I stepped out, all eyes were looking away from the door toward Mandy, who stood on the far side, facing back to the gathering. Voices were shrill. "What did they say, Mandy?" "Did you get the transfer?" "I'll bet you told the bastards, Mandy!" "Tell us what happened!" Constance, pale and fragile-looking, cupping her chin with delicate fingers, gazed imploringly at her friend.

Mandy was beaded with sweat like a boxer between rounds. Her eyes widened briefly as I appeared. Others caught her change of face and, turning, saw me. All voices hushed; the only sound came from a tractor running somewhere outside of the fence.

Mandy abruptly turned and headed out in the direction of the gym. I kept her in sight as I edged through the group. No one said a word or tried to stop me—everyone just made way, stepping back, lowering their heads as though by looking at the ground they could not themselves be seen. In twos and threes they drifted noiselessly across the grass, back to the obscurity of their deserted work stations on the lawn and in the gardens.

I followed along the winding, flower-bordered sidewalk behind Mandy. Beyond her the campus seemed lifeless. It was an oddly peaceful afternoon in which the tractor's hum was still the only sound. Mandy obviously had some destination in mind, but I had no idea of her intentions. At the far corner of the gymnasium she turned and was out of sight. As I rounded the gym she was walking briskly toward the tool house, which stood well back from the living units between the greenhouse and the potting sheds. And still, no one else was in sight.

To my surprise, Mandy stopped when I called out to her; she turned toward me, elbows tight against her waist, and waited for me to catch up. A vague quality of lost hope had overtaken the stormy features of her outrageous anger, and in her flat-footed stance there was a mark of resignation; but she unflinchingly hefted the grass shears in an outstretched hand like a preacher hammering home the promise of awful judgement with a Bible. Her face was drawn, but her voice was fiercely resonant: "I'm puttin' those clippers in the tool shed where they belongs, Rosen, then I'm gonna go lock myself in my room."

The show was, indeed, suddenly and quite calmly, over. Mandy knew that she would be consigned to lock-up in the "hole" for many days. She could cope with that: how many times had she already disdainfully outlasted the darkness, the limited rations, and the thinly cushioned, rock-hard bed of cement in Isolation? For the moment, though, in her unyielding way, she was yet in charge. Adroitly holding herself above any more active exercise of authority by me, she would take herself to her room in Homestead Cottage to await the inevitable punishment. To allow her such independence could be less disturbing to the institution than if I were to officiously accompany her; there was no need for me to prove a point of personal or institutional might.

"Yes, that's the way it has to be, Mandy," I said softly.

Without further words, Mandy lowered the shears, turned, and resumed her trip to the tool shed.

Looking after her, I became aware of the sun's heat heavy on my shoulders. My shirt stuck to my body, and I was very thirsty. Slowly, and without enthusiasm, I started back to the administration building, stopping at the corner of the gym to loosen my tie and remove my coat. It was still only Tuesday and there were nine more inmates to be seen by the Classification Committee. That work had to be done, and I had to return to it. Before the meeting could recommence, the committee and its records would have to be moved from the ravaged conference room to some other workspace. My reluctant colleagues were going to have to stay here beyond quitting time tonight.

With a backward glance I saw Mandy, sinewy and hunched, enter the tool shed. There came the sharp clatter of the grass shears landing on the workbench where she threw them. For a moment she stood still, her head drooping; then she reached down, took the ends of her faded sash in both of her hands, and held them to her face.

The perverse pleasure that she took from her outburst in the conference room was abysmal in its impending cost, which would be the prolonged, coldly enforced, excruciating void of the sight . . . of the voice . . . of the touch . . . of her gentle friend.

Turning Points

As in the free world, there is a pecking order behind prison walls. On top, so to speak, are the aggressors who prey remorselessly in a variety of ways on others lower down. They run rackets of loans, drugs, sex, or protection for their own aggrandizement and psychopathic satisfaction. They are without conscience, can smile and be charming when they wish, but they know nothing of love, empathy, goodness, and beauty; their attention is exclusively on themselves and the fulfillment of their selfish desires. They are the least human, the most dangerous.

On the bottom are the weak, inadequate "mice," who slink to and from their cells trying not to be noticed, trying to avoid the aggressors and escape danger. Some of these will sell their bodies, their canteen draws, cigarettes, or menial services to gain "friendship," the protection of a stronger inmate, hoping for some niche of security in a groveling existence.

Between the predators and the inadequates is the vast group of inmates who are of neither extreme. Their offenses are not characteristically rapacious or sadistic; in fact, they usually abhor aggressive and deviant crimes. For whatever reasons, buried in soul and psyche, their felonies have dealt with bad checks, stolen property, embezzlement, even robbery, and may have been interwoven with alcoholism or other addictions and an instability of purpose and direction. Within their make-ups are psychic patterns of discontent and jealously, of angry self-righteousness, depression, or extreme dependency mingled with, and sometimes dominating, their healthier qualities and good intentions. It is more often that the hopeful prison purpose of "reform" is achieved among the members of this group than the others.

Clyde Connor (A-37557), neither a psychopath nor a feeble mouse, was not one to put a kink in the prison pecking order. He was of average height and weight and of reasonably good posture. His hair was brown, slightly curly; he had pale blue eyes and his light skin had a scattering of freckles. He was meticulous about his appearance, always kept his clothes clean, and was very careful to bathe and shave regularly–as he wished others would do. Seldom did he smile, for he was chronically "down," but on the rare occasions when he had contact with a counselor or other official he was pleasant, soft-spoken, and polite.

His crimes had been against property, not people–no sexual derangement or violence. Admittedly he had done a lot of stealing, but he did not regard himself as a criminal; he thought of himself as a "loser" or as unlucky, his life controlled by others or by inescapable "circumstances." And so his thefts were rationalized at the time–the often drunken time–of their planning and execution. Now, too late, he thought of himself as pretty stupid for having pilfered telephones–he'd hit a "route" of pay phones throughout central California–and for fencing stolen property.

Very much as he had been on the streets, Connor was a loner in this catchment of 5,000 whose names were numbers. He was too bright to take up with the passive, boring "jerks" whose conversations tended to be fabrications of macho exploits in the free world. Like self-styled Robin Hoods, they lied about making out with a gorgeous chick or supporting an invalid mother and pretended, especially to themselves, that once back out they would set things straight with someone who had finked on them. These were mouthy, "subhuman creeps" whom Connor avoided. And, since he was not big enough to be much of a fighter who could establish for himself a private space of invulnerability with his dukes, he was careful to avoid the aggressive toughs at the upper end of the scale.

In this place Connor's cautions and aversions were not entirely unreasonable, but a more serious reality was that, when you came right down to it, there weren't many people of *any* kind *anywhere* whom Connor liked much. He was an intelligent man who intended to be honest with himself but, like most of us, he was not fully successful at this: he had his blind spots.

For instance, he was compulsively critical and intolerant of the shortcomings that he perceived in most people. He did a silent and continuous burn about the dishonesty of those in unions or government or about the privileges of the well-to-do. The insensitive or arrogant treatment of some ordinary person by one of power put him in a rage.

On the other hand, he had compassion for the little guy–a guy like himself, say–doing his best. But if ever even a little guy let himself get too fat, eat crudely, absentmindedly trip over something because he was walking like a gawk, ask dumb questions, or scratch himself in public, that was it: cross him off as a Sorry Slob. Once in a long while he might wonder to himself, "Hey, dude, you're so smart–why ain't you rich?" But that came to very little and did not lead to much self-understanding, for it was much easier and safer to concentrate on the faults of others.

Somehow, in the course of a miserable childhood, a drunken, bar-hopping, sleeparound mother had taught Clyde Connor the basics of right and wrong. Who knows how it happened, but it had. Still, one might wonder, if that had led to his being a man of conscience, how could he be in big trouble for stealing, for being a "common thief" (a phrase that had stung when spoken by his sentencing judge)?

Not only had the mother's lessons stuck, but some rigid-to-the-core, defensive part of him went way beyond self-regulation to a constant, unyielding, angry, unforgiving expectation that all others, too, should toe the mark of righteousness, which, of course, hardly anyone ever did to his satisfaction. Then, quirkily, he would twist the failures of all those around him to a justification of his hitting on them as a respite from his own treadmill life of intermittent unemployment, need for money, black moods, heavy drinking, unhappiness with his wife, and what-all. It was a feeble rationalization, and in his stronger moments he vaguely knew it; so when he was finally sent up he had to grudgingly admit to himself that, as the rules went out there, he was not imprisoned unjustly, just . . . damn unluckily. But he still didn't like the hotshot barons of riches and power . . .

Connor was fortunate in having a job as a time clerk in the prison furniture factory, and he was glad for that; sort of like a crossword puzzle, it was something to do. And he got good work reports because his recordkeeping was always neat and accurate; but he shrugged off the compliments, somehow converting them to downers, saying, "When you've got a job to do, you're supposed to do it the best you can. What do they think I am, a nut? They so seldom see a job done well in here that they go out of their gourds when they find somebody who does things right." Secretly, though, it did feel good to get a pat on the head, and–who knows?–good work reports might look good to the parole board too.

Otherwise, Connor did hard time. In his cellblock the cells, measuring six by eight feet, were sturdily stacked five tiers high. When built they had been intended for single occupancy, but that had not lasted long; second bunks were welded in and you took whom you were assigned as a cellmate. "That's one example of inhumanly cruel punishment," Connor angrily mused.

His cellmate, Slim Jorgensen, was a gangly, foul-mouthed extrovert with bad teeth and nauseating armpits. When he did wash or shave he was proficient at spraying everything at the washbasin-end of the cell, including Connor's pillow, with lather and dirty water. His use of the toilet was revolting; it was a great joke to him if his stream overshot the bowl. As far as possible Connor ignored this human wreck, but not without gritting his teeth and getting knots in his belly. He spent hours lying on his bunk, face to the wall, grateful for a set of headphones that gave a humdrum selection of four radio programs.

He tried to read some, but that was scant escape—he had trouble keeping his mind on it. Some people made models, did leatherwork, played a guitar, sketched or wrote, but he took no pleasure in any of these things. Sometimes he wrote a letter, but that usually didn't take long, because what was there to say?

One day Jorgensen got busted for badmouthing an officer on the yard and was sent to the "shelf" for two weeks. Having the cell to himself was like a drug-free high for Connor. He spent the first evening making the place spotless with soap and water, euphoric in his solitude.

Once in a long, long while, when there was a sunny weekend, he might go to the athletic field and stretch out on a bleacher. This was a reprieve from the cell, and the sun's rays felt pretty good. The smell of the salt air from the nearby bay purged his nose and throat of the unpleasant odors that seemed to exude from the steel cages and cheerless buildings. He was always careful to pick a spot that was not too far from a correctional officer—a safety precaution. No inmate rumble was likely to start right under a CO's nose.

A few officers were surly, mean devils, but most of them were bearable. It was easiest to treat them all as The Man, a living symbol of one's loss of freedom and the state's determination to keep it that way, but if you backed off and looked at it good, a little more charitably than was customary, you had to admit that they must do something right: they were only in here for forty hours a week. In between times they went home from the job to wives and kids—their own pack of joys and sorrows, which was more than he could do. Anyhow, he felt safer to be in sight of one of them, and contrary to the inmate code, if push came to shove his tenuous loyalty would probably be with the COs.

For all of his intelligence, the man was lost—pathetically, abandoned-little-boy lost. He had never learned, never figured out, ways to take hold of life—not just in prison, but anywhere—and create satisfaction for himself, let alone for others. What he did not see—this was his big blind spot—was his trait of waiting for someone else to make things happen. And so this boy/man with a good brain, a sense of right and wrong, and a willingness to work when somebody told him what to do was in two prisons: the gray, granite-walled one confining him with all of the others in their pecking order; and another one within himself, unseen, uncomprehended, a confinement resulting from his own passivity.

Clyde Connor's marriage, surprisingly, was still intact. When it had become clear that he was going to be locked up for as long as five years, he had told his wife that she should divorce him. But she had refused. She'd endured a whole lot up to this point—like his absences from home without explanation for days in a row—and wasn't giving up now. He was a sheetrocker by trade, and when he worked he made good money, but too often the money did not reach home. Between bouts of drinking he worked hard, sometimes for weeks at a time. He'd spend the evenings with Clara and their little girl, Cathy; they'd play cards, take in a movie, go for walks, sometimes visit her relatives.

Clara was pleased by his tenderness with the baby. Even in his moody spells he was good to the baby. He had been honorable enough to marry Clara when she became pregnant—hadn't wanted to get tied down like that, but "you don't make babies and abandon them." Now Clara often felt, without jealousy, that Cathy meant more to him than she did. She saw the goodness in him, a certain lonely vulnerability and, when it popped out, a sense of humor and a sweet laugh that were, for her, worth waiting for. She was drawn to him much like a dog is faithful to a dissolute master.

It was a teeter-totter relationship. There were long times devoid of any laughter when Clara's easy-going, optimistic nature aggravated Clyde unreasonably: "How can she be such a pollyanna? Why can't she see that there isn't that much to feel good about?"

Clara was so steady, always quietly there, almost never reproachful. She had a round, open face, dark, smiley eyes, straw-colored hair combed straight back to a short pony tail. Plumpish, she dressed frugally in clothes bought at rummage sales, but she was always clean and she had a wonderful smile. From her, Clyde received more tenderness than he'd ever known from anyone, and for that he often felt guilty: "God, she sticks with me and I'm not worth it. I get so much from her and don't give nothin' back." Such thoughts then might lead to a drinking bout: "If you can't fix it, drown it."

Connor wrote—when he wrote—two kinds of letters to Clara. The first would go like this: "Thank you for your loyalty to me. I've never earned it, but you've stuck by me and I don't know why. I am just living to get out of this dreadful place and make it up to you for all of the times I've let you down." As he wrote he would come alive, knowing that, in spite of his fault-finding and irritability, this woman cared about him, remained faithful. With an exciting fantasy of their physical closeness, he would drop the letter in the mailbox and risk a walk in the sunshine or watch a game of chess in the cellblock. He looked forward to Clara's next visit; all would come well between them.

Clara visited the prison once a month. The round-trip by bus took a full day. They could be together in the usually crowded visiting room for no longer than an hour at most. It was agreed that she would not bring Cathy. Connor could not bear to have the child know that there were places like this where bad men were locked up and that he was in one of them.

Still, contrary to such longings born of his loneliness, as Clara's visiting day approached, Connor would find himself growing vaguely uncomfortable. He knew that she would bring him cigarettes, which he needed; she would leave a little money in his canteen account, and she might bring some pictures. He wanted these things, was grateful for them; yet he had a feeling of muted dread.

After their first few minutes, he would be at a loss to make conversation. When she reached out to hold his hand he felt an ill-defined discomfort, secretly wishing to pull back, but forcing himself to stay in her grasp. She would smile at him warmly, waiting, coaxing him to speak. Her motherly plainness, her sweetness, her pervasive expectancy made him feel closed in. He struggled for animation, to say things that would tell her that he cared, to make her feel loved and appreciated. But his mind ran away; blankly, he stared at the bare wall above her head, avoiding her eyes, thinking that "in a few minutes she'll be leaving for the bus . . . " Palms sweating, he was impatient for the visit to come to an end and to have her gone.

Then he would return to his job or the cell out of sorts with himself, glad to have the goodies that Clara had brought and yet, damn it, feeling relieved of her closeness. After a few days of troubling ambivalence, he would send her a letter of a second type in which he gently wrote, "Thanks for making that long trip to see me. I hope you had a good trip home and that Cathy was glad to have you back. Thanks for the cigarettes and money that you brought. I really needed them, but I hate it that you have to work to do it." Then, bluntly, he went on as he often had before: "Clara, you should leave me. You are too good for me. You should not be wasting your life waiting for me—no one should have to endure what I have put you through. I have always let you down and it doesn't seem to change. I think that we should call it quits and you should not visit me again. It will be hard for me, but I think it would be for the best."

Tearfully reading and rereading the letter, Clara felt even more committed to this man whose wavering mystery had always drawn him to her.

Then, in another week or two, Clyde's discomfort with Clara would be overshadowed by loneliness again. He forgot about the closed-in feeling and thought only of her love, her generosity and sweetness. He wrote of how much he missed her: "I can't make it without you. Please, please visit me again soon." And she always did. It was a cycle that had been repeated a dozen times.

One night a week, Conner was allowed to leave his cell to go to the AA meeting. He'd signed up not simply because it might look good to the parole board; for too long he'd denied that his drinking binges were a problem, "But," he came to think, "most other people don't drink like that. . . . I'll take a crack at it. At least it'll be a few hours outa the funky cell and away from shit-ass Jorgensen."

The group was run by two volunteers who came out from the city every week, never failed. They didn't present themselves as hot stuff like shrinks or preachers—just a couple of drunks who knew that they had to stay on the wagon if they were to survive. Making no big deal of it, they were open about what a mess their lives had been and how, even now, they were just one drink away from personal chaos. Always cautious and critical, Conner was uncharacteristically impressed with them, especially the older one, Tom Riley. Years later, looking back, Conner often wondered, "How was I ever so lucky as to meet Tom Riley? Without ever sayin' much that guy helped me get my head straight. If it hadn't been for him, who knows where I'd be now?"

Riley was a big, kindly, self-effacing yet confident man who seemed to listen as carefully with his friendly eyes as with his ears. There was a serenity about him—it was as if he had passed through some terrible experience like a death march and had barely survived, but out of it he'd got a hold on an inner peace; he'd learned a deep patience with the events of his own life and a nonjudgemental acceptance of the troubles of other men.

Connor had never before felt as if he counted or amounted to much with any man. There had been a whole string of men around his mother's house, but none of them had much to do with him, not much that was good anyway. But Riley was something else. For starters he didn't have to go inside those walls week after week; it wasn't as if he was paid to show up to a job like a state employee. He came there because he gave a damn. "He could have brushed me off as just another crook, but that guy honestly believed I was an okay person, important, you know!"

It was in their private talks following the group (Conner never opened up much in group), sometimes over a cup of coffee, that Conner started laying his guts out to Riley, speaking nonstop of Clara and his little girl, of his drinking episodes and his stupid stealing and how he wanted things to be better. He'd never talked so much before. But he'd never had a listener like Tom Riley before either.

Not that trust of Riley (or the ability to trust) came all at once. There were always roadblocks and setbacks. Old patterns didn't just fade away. Like the day when big-time convict Caryl Chessman had been offed in the gas chamber. Conner didn't like Chessman or the crimes he'd done, but he hated the state for executing him. That night, Conner had dumped all over Riley.

"You come in here every week all smiles and kindness, ready to 'save' a con, but you're part of 'society' out there, man. You all support the state in locking people up in a rathole like this for years and years and even rubbing out the worst of us. The government calls it justice, but it's murder, man, and every free man's a part of it." Conner exploded on and on; years and years of venom poured out, and Riley caught it all, quietly listening, making no effort to dissuade or denigrate, never lashing back as a man of lesser understanding most likely would. Finally, hoarse and spent, near tears, Conner stomped out, saying, "I'll never be back here! You 'good citizen' hypocrites are even worse than cons!"

But the next week Conner was back, awkward, showing a sheepish, somehow boyish grin. "I'm sorry I unloaded on you last week, Mr. Riley. You don't deserve the crap I handed out. I didn't know I had that much evil in me! When I cooled off, I saw that your putting up with me without pounding my head off or turning me in to The Man or even just telling me to shut up was the greatest thing that ever happened to me. I've never felt this clean before. 'That man really is my friend,' I said. I never felt like this before! You ain't gonna give up on me now, are ya?" he asked, looking with unwavering warmth and directness into the big man's eyes with an almost desperate plea for reassurance.

Riley shook his shaggy head with calm understanding, saying with bedrock simplicity, "Thanks, Clyde. I'm glad you're back."

It was a major turning point.

On returning to his desk from the mess hall one noon, Connor was met by his freeman supervisor, who told him there was a message for him from the captain's office. "You're supposed to go over there right away."

Going pale, round eyes flashing fright, Connor said, "What for, man? You know what for?" But the civilian knew nothing more and shook his head as he sat down at his desk to write out a pass while making a sadistic joke: "I supposed you've screwed up in the cellblock some way!"

As Connor crossed the herringboned, red-brick yard from the factory to the captain's office, he frantically searched his mind: "What have I done wrong? What rule could I have violated? Maybe somebody's trying to set me up, trying to mess with me. Wait a minute. . . . Could this have something to do with Jorgensen? Maybe that obnoxious son-of-a-bitch has contraband in the cell, maybe in my stuff!" His panic changed to anger and he prepared to defend himself.

The captain's office was a well-lighted suite on ground level facing a poorly tended patio, which was euphemistically called "Garden Beautiful," but which was grotesque with withered plants, a corrosion-crippled fountain, and the clumsy, misshapen animal statues once fashioned by some now-forgotten inmate "artist." Inside, four blue-denim-clad clerks sat at desks in the main room. Theirs was a cushy work assignment, for they were in a position to know the official scoop on the big things going on in the joint. Proctor, the chief clerk, was one of the cons whom Connor knew in AA and who seemed all right. He nodded for Connor to take a seat and gave him a reassuring, thumbs-up gesture. That was a relief, but it didn't solve the mystery. One pretty sure thing though: whatever was going on, it couldn't be anything about Clara or Cathy; any bad news of them would come through the chaplain's office.

The captain was a red-faced, big-bellied Irishman of many year's prison employment who was known among the cons as a tough dude. With Connor he was neither cold nor cordial. Matter-of-factly, keeping Connor standing in front of the desk, he stated, "Connor, you're wanted as a witness in a federal trial about to start in Los Angeles. You will be released to two marshals first thing tomorrow morning. They'll take you down there, where you'll be held in the county jail until you are called to testify in court, and when that is completed you'll be brought back here. Got that?"

"Yes sir, I've got it," Connor answered, relieved and holding back a smile. What a surprise and what a weight off his shoulders this was! He was aware of a pending federal case about which he had some information. A lawyer had come to talk with him about it weeks ago, but Connor didn't know until now that he would be called as a witness. This was going to be a break from the gray-walled routine! Even staying a few nights in the Los Angeles County Jail would be a welcome change. Vacations are relative to what is being vacated.

Leaning over the counter on his way out of the office, he said to the chief clerk, "Hey, Proctor, tomorrow night at AA tell Mr. Riley why I'm not there, will you, man?"

"Sure, man, I'll tell him you had to make a business trip to look after some of your vast financial holdings down south. Have a good trip. Don't do nothin' I wouldn't do!"

It was a long but pleasant drive to L.A. The feds were neither hard-nosed nor frivolous with him. Riding alone in the locked rear seat, Connor was able to relax and take in the sights along the inland highway, which he'd traveled a good many times before. All along, in Stockton, Modesto, and Fresno he glimpsed places he remembered: the Silver Dollar Bar, Judy's Joint, the Roxy Theater, the Fresno County Jail—"Oops, forget that one! I can't wait to be back out here again. It will be different. No more county jail, though. Not for me. It will be Mr. Straight, man." These were his thoughts. "And I'll make it up to Clara. I've got to. We've got a kid to raise."

He was in L.A. for three nights. The jail was a zoo, but he was able to avoid any serious problems. After less than an hour in court on the fourth day they started the return trip mid-afternoon, reaching Oakland at 10 p.m. Rather than go on to the prison at that hour, the marshals decided to put up for the night, placing Connor in the jail atop the Alameda County Courthouse as an overnight "guest." To the jailers they said with sly laughter, "We're going out for a little well-earned R and R. Tell your reliefs not to look for us too early in the morning, fellahs. . . . "

The overnight delay was okay with Connor. He felt fortunate to be placed in a clean, single cell rather than a crowded holding tank as he had been down south. He didn't have to deal with the curiosity and hostility of a new batch of human trash. He even had a shower; it was almost as good as a night at a Hilton. Not that he'd ever stayed in a Hilton.

Connor was awakened from a sound sleep at 6 a.m. by an agitated, very hyper jailer who told him to hurry up, goddamn it, and get dressed. He was hustled out of the cell through a security door and into the booking room by the officer, who seemed under great pressure to get a lot done at once. Two sleepy deputies sat at cramped desks in the far corner mouthing stained coffee cups, staring at papers in front of them in a flutter of cigarette ashes, paying no attention to the harried jailer or to Connor. Connor saw nothing of his escorting federal agents, who should be here if he were being checked out. "Maybe the jokers phoned in or something; the way they talked last night, I didn't expect to see them before mid-morning," he thought sourly to himself.

It looked like some big change in plans; however, he was resigned, if not happily so, to having his life controlled for the convenience of others. You ask no questions because you won't get a straight answer anyway.

Unlocking a small drawer in a whole rack of drawers, the jailer shoved Connor his cigarettes and few other personal things across the table, had him sign a receipt for them, then impatiently motioned him to write his signature on a line in a big, leather-bound book that lay on a sloping, stand-up counter. "Okay, this way," said the jailer, and led him to the elevator through a passageway with a locked steel door at either end.

Still not fully alert, Connor was resentful at having his sleep interrupted; he thought that the jailer looked like a stupid, short-eared jackrabbit hopping around with little coherence; for whatever reason, the job seemed to be too much for him. In a pattern of thought typical for him, he disdained the officer's incompetence, but things were moving too rapidly for him to dwell on the point. As the doors slid open, the officer, with a brusque nod of his head and a flip of his thumb, motioned him onto the elevator. The doors hushed closed and suddenly he was alone.

"What's happening?" Connor asked himself aloud as the car made a twelve-story, air-cushioned drop to ground level, where the sliding doors automatically opened. Hesitating, he stepped cautiously into the dimly lit, tunnel-like, block-long hallway with city streets showing through the double glass doors at either end. He waited expectantly to hear a phone ring and to have a security official step out of a cubicle and confront him. But there was only silence, no sign of life; the corridor was deserted.

Disbelieving, he looked both ways again, turned left, and walked slowly north to the glass doors, which he found unlocked. Pushing through, he stepped out onto the sidewalk and tentatively took in the empty street.

It began to sink in—it didn't make sense, but there was only one explanation: by some error that stupid screw had turned him loose. "Jesus. I'm out of there! I'm out of there! Now what should I do?" On an empty stomach this was making him feel weak and dizzy. Pain throbbed through his groin and he felt incontinent.

Hanging on, steadying himself for a moment in the fresh bracing air, his head began to work. The cement sidewalk was free under his feet! His impulse was to shout and run like a kid on the last day of school, to get out of there before someone figured out what happened. "All I gotta do is move outta here!" Then, thinking of his ill-cut prison dungarees, he cautioned himself, "Wait, wait . . . You gotta be cool.

Don't draw attention to yourself. Walk slow, man, and figure what to do."

At the bus stop on the corner he leaned against the back of the empty concrete bench, lit up a cigarette, and made like a working man heading for an early morning job. "God, where should I go? I've got no money. I can't even make a long distance call to Clara." Which would do no good anyway since she was 300 miles away and had no car.

Without quite identifying it, he watched the round, red sun come up over the hills to the east and felt its increasing warmth on his face. Across the way in the neatly tended gardens of a public park glowed a long bank of flowers, white daisies in bright bloom. They seemed strikingly crisp and clean against dark green leaves and made him think of Clara. Damn it! She had always wished they could have a garden of their own with some white daisies. He should have had the decency to see that such a simple wish had been fulfilled, he thought fleetingly. "Hell, why am I thinking of this stuff now. I've got to make a move!" He inhaled strenuously on the cigarette and expelled a grey cloud into the morning air.

"I'm not supposed to be out here, that's for sure. Someone has made one hell of a mistake. I could make a dash for it and be out of here by the time they figure it out. . . . "

But some restraining sensibility held him back, saying that to run would not bring freedom. "If I make a run for it I'll have to be on the run forever, and even then they'll get me, the bastards'll get me in time. . . . "

The faltering "someone" who'd mistakenly let him out had to be that stupid jailer, and as he came to mind Connor was consumed with compulsive rage at the incompetence of people such as that dude in responsible places.

"What I should do is burn that stupid pig. All I've got to do is find a cop, turn myself in, and I'm a hero and that idiot up there will be out of a job; he could be hunting employment in a different line of work for a long, long time."

But then, more thoughtfully, he mused, "Hell, I don't even know that poor fool. They've got him in over his head up there. I don't really have anything against him. . . . "

"So, say I turn him in and cook his goose . . . where does that get me? Nobody at the joint is going to pat me on the head and say, 'Oh, you fine cat—you are too good to be in here—we'll send you home at once.' That kook has probably got a wife and kids and if he loses his lousy job over this he could be in a hell of a mess. I could take off from here without turning him in, but I probably can't even get out of town, and even if I could, I'd be in the soup a whole lot worse than him. All's he'd get is fired, and when they caught me I'd get another year's time or more!"

The morning air was out of his consciousness now along with the warmth of the sun and the crisp white flowers blooming across the street. "This is a screwed-up deal, but for once it is no fault of mine! I can set it straight—and save that knothead's job for him; or I can make it worse for both of us."

He lit a second cigarette. None of the options offered much. He desperately hated prison and longed to be free, but he knew—sometimes his head worked right and he KNEW—that there were no shortcuts off through a city park to a getaway even when a jailer had screwed up.

Inmate Connor, temporarily free, took one last drag of smoke, flipped the cigarette into the gutter and, with a resurgence of the sick feeling, walked slowly back to the long hallway and the elevator.

Stepping out at the top floor he pushed the call button at the side of the security door for The Man. Amidst the metallic clatter of bronze keys turning in heavy locks, the rabbit face appeared, skewing into an angry question mark. "Well, asshole, what are you doing back here—forget your undies?"

In an emotional montage of contempt, anger, disappointment, and yes, strange as it seems, pity, Connor exploded: "Don't 'asshole' me, you simple fart. I don't know who you thought—or think—I am, but you've let the wrong sucker out. My name is Connor. Conner! I'm in here on a 'hold' for the feds who are transporting me to 'Q.' Unless you've got special powers from the Pope or the parole board or God Almighty you have blown it really big."

The question-mark face faded yellow. Nothing so bloodless could remain living for long. Elbowing past the jailer through the open door, Connor said, "I can't believe I'm doing this. You ought to lose your job, but you won't have to. Not this time. I'm a sucker for poor dumb shits, and you qualify. Put me back in my private cell; I'll stay quiet, won't say nothing about your unbelievable screw-up if you don't. After all, it makes me look pretty stupid too—Christ! Begging my way back in here! . . . "

Neither man said more as they moved through the corridor to the booking room and beyond to the empty cell from which Connor had so recently been summoned. Looking through the bars of the cell door as it kachunked shut, the jailer's eyes pleaded disbelief. Incoherent, he could only utter, "Jesus, God . . . I . . . you . . . you ain't Conroy? I thought you was . . . uh, Conroy . . . ," and then he turned like a shabby puppet dangling limply at the end of a single string and faded along the corridor.

Connor slumped upright on the bunk, slamming his back against the flaking green steel wall, and closed his eyes. His heart pounded as though he'd climbed the twelve stories two steps at a time. Images jerked through his head like home movies running backwards: the funky screw, the cushioned ride in the elevator, the deserted hallway and city streets, the rising sun, the taunting freedom of a city park, and his return–his goddamn voluntary return!–to jail where the feds would come and get him. And they would never know. The lousy bastards would never know. Which somehow, oddly, put him one up on them.

He wanted to rake his throat bloody with a scream, "Screw the world!" and to rage around the cell and cry and beat the bars and wrench the toilet from the wall, flooding water down the hall . . .

But he stayed rigid on the bunk, teeth, eyes, and guts clamped tight, knots of muscle and blue veins showing ugly on his neck, and ground his hands into the jailhouse blankets.

By afternoon he would be back in the frightful, sickening joint where this forty-minute episode would be remembered as a dream, one so wrenching as to demand sharing, but whose climax–whose turning point–was too square, too "straight," to risk an open telling to any there but one. In two more nights he'd see his friend again. Tom Riley could be told the story. He'd listen, by God, nod his graying head, be glad, and understand.

Power Makes Its Own Rules

You hear some strange stories in prison. Many of them are self-serving, designed to gain a favor or special attention as well as to stake out the teller's ego territory. Often what such tales yield their tellers is no more than bored tolerance or curt dismissal.

I was particularly intrigued, however, with a story told me by one San Quentin lifer. He did not bring it up on his own in some attempt to influence me, for I had invited it. And his crime was of such a serious nature that he would be spending the rest of his life locked up; telling me the yarn could bear him no special advantage beyond congeniality.

The man—paradoxically, his name was Straight—was not one whom I regularly saw, but in the absence of his own counselor I had been asked to do a report of some sort on him whose purpose I have since forgotten. Scanning his thick file before meeting him, I found that it was a record of years and years of offenses graduating from juvenile delinquency to adult crime and finally to the sordid, skid-row murder that put him away for the rest of his life.

He had served time in the prisons of at least three other states, and when I saw that the first of these had been the penitentiary of my home state way back in the days of prohibition, my ears picked up. I wanted to hear what he could tell me about the inside of that old place; it had awed me as a boy, for it stood fearsome and austere, like a red brick castle behind a formidable granite wall, ironically wedged between the tracks of a major railroad and the town's main street, along which I had ridden with my parents on several occasions.

In our meeting, the wizened, middle-aged man, a sunken-cheeked, ugly-toothed, generally unattractive bundle of human failure was hard to deal with; as though driven by a tightly wound spring he talked on and on about the faults of others—public figures, Christians, bankers, the police, other inmates, prison officials, anyone but himself. It was clear that his garrulity was the one crusty defense holding him somewhat together, and so I was reasonably patient with it. As our interview wound down in its official purpose, though, I risked a further outpouring of words in order to indulge my curiosity: "I see you did time in the prison of my home state," I said.

"Which state is that?"

I named the state and asked, "What kind of a place was that? Was it a tough place to do time?"

At first, oddly, the man seemed at a loss for words; his eyes made brief questioning contact with mine, then quickly looked away as though he were searching up recollections from some inner repository.

"Yeah, I done time there. It was a bum rap. I'd been travelin' through the state with a carnival. The buggers went off and left me when I got drunk and passed out one night. In the morning I got busted for stealin' something that I never stole, and they sent me to the joint."

I didn't want to get off onto another everything's-wrong-with-everybody-but-me kind of tale, and luckily I was able to steer him to reminiscing instead of simply complaining. As the man picked among his memories, he spoke with a degree of detail surprising from one who otherwise seemed of rather dull intellect, and after a rather general description of the old place, one thing leading to another, he came up with a story that I could hardly believe, and yet it seemed unlikely that this peevish raconteur could have fabricated it.

"'Most everybody in that place—all us cons—knowed it weren't just the inmates that was crooks," Straight said. "You bet we knowed that! Like there was this still in the basement of the prison theatre where some of the brass was makin' moonshine. Lots of it. (Right off, I wondered at the man's use of the word "theatre," which seemed pretty grandiose for a prison building, but in this, as with other details, he proved accurate.)

"They done it with the help of some of their goody-goody finks, o' course. So ever' week after the afternoon count, when most ever'body but a few goody-goodies was locked up in their cells, there'd come to the sally port in the east wall this here big, black, seven-passenger Packard touring sedan. It was some car for them days! I seen it myself, all enclosed with leather side-curtains with little isinglass windows. It had a freeman driver o' course, and the officer on the gate let him drive right on in and go slow across the yard to the back end of the theatre."

Straight said that he'd never seen what went on there, but "what ever'body knowed was that a coupla trusties carried jugs o' moonshine up from the basement and poured 'em into metal tanks in the place where the rear seat was took outa the car." When the tanks were filled, the freeman driver eased the vehicle, rear-end-heavy with liquid cargo, back to the sally port for inspection against some inmate's sneak departure and was then allowed to drive out and away.

"You know where that load o' booze went?" my outraged historian asked without waiting for an answer. "Why, it went forty miles down the road to this here high-livin' miners' town, and there it was delivered to the alley door of the Mint Pool Hall—what used to be the Mint Bar; that's what they called it before the start of prohibition. And the Mint Pool Hall was owned—now get this—the old Mint Bar, now a pool hall, was owned by a feller named Mort Driscoll who was the big brother of Sam Driscoll, who was the warden of the prison! That's how that worked."

"You're telling me, Straight," I said, "that the warden was making moonshine inside his own prison and peddling it to his brother, who owned a speakeasy in a nearby town?"

"That's the God's truth," said Straight in a triumph of conviction.

Actually, the production of a little alcohol is a perennial, though of course forbidden, endeavor of prison inmates, so the presence of such a sophisticated device as a still was remotely credible. But the enterprise here described was neither that of a novice nor of small scale. It was hard for me to instantly believe that a prison warden would be complicit in such a hypocritical, not to mention illegal, venture, but how else could it flourish? Straight's "facts" pieced together pretty well, and I was eager to check them out somehow.

It was not until some years later, however, that I learned beyond a shadow of a doubt that certain incongruous characteristics of the warden, as well as some singular aspects of the western state's history, made the preposterous tale seem, well, quite likely.

By the time that I had a chance to seriously research the story, the San Quentin lifer had been buried in a pauper's grave, and Warden Sam Driscoll and his principal prison associates had been dead and gone for even longer—not that I thought that any of them would have copped to the tale if confronted with it. Making a trip to the town of Cottonwood, where the prison still stands, I found a handful of old-timers whose childhoods had overlapped Driscoll's final years. Their recollections of Warden Driscoll were largely fragmentary and secondhand, but I was intrigued by their inadvertent repetition of such words and phrases as: "colorful" . . . "controversial" . . . "a big man" . . . "quite a politician" . . . "ruthless, he was ruthless" . . . "he ran this town." I seemed to be on the brink of more of a story than I'd dreamt of.

There is no comprehensive biography of Warden Sam Driscoll; to learn of him it was necessary to reconnoiter between the printed lines of official records and to grub through the prolific accounts of his activities to be found in contemporary newspapers. Fortunately, he was a lively source of copy for the days' journalists; depending on the seat and the political bent of the reporting publication, there are quite contrasting representations to be found of the man and his activities.

But of these divergencies it is safe to say that the man's nature was so many-faceted that various observers, whether friend or foe, could very well see different qualities and respond in quite differing ways according to their own viewpoints, representing him as a gifted giant or a scheming villain. The engrossing challenge for me was to winnow out a reasonably accurate portrait of the man from the conflicting old accounts. Incidentally, very early on I was encouraged in my search when I verified that the warden had indeed had an older brother who was a bar owner—or pool hall proprietor, depending on the year—in the infamous mining town just as Straight had said.

Like so many youngsters of the post-Civil War years, Sammy Driscoll had quit school and left the eastern home of his widowed mother at the age of sixteen, heading off to independence, big-game hunting, and other adventure in a far-west territory where he first found work as a surveyor's helper in Yellowstone Park and then as a deputy sheriff.

When, as a deputy, he delivered two Chinese railroad laborers (convicted of the illegal possession and sale of opium) to the primitive territorial prison, he was struck by the beauty of the lockup's location in a broad mountain valley, a hunter's paradise that he could not resist. Quitting the sheriff's job at once, he signed on as a prison guard in a move that led to much more than bountiful hunting opportunities, for there soon evolved an unusual and lengthy career encompassing power, influential friendships, mixed motives, wealth, renown, and controversy.

In 1889, two years after Driscoll became a prison guard, Congress made a state of the territory that the prison served. Initially strapped for operating funds, the new state's officials proposed to contract for the private operation of the penitentiary as one way to husband their resources. Anticipating this development, Driscoll had formed an alliance with a friend and fellow prison employee by the name of Dan Daniels. Daniels, having earlier been the local county sheriff, was well-known and well-liked. He had a good reputation, a string of racehorses and a modest savings account. These were assets sufficient to enable the partners to formalize a business arrangement called the

Double D Corporation (from the first letter of their last names) with themselves as sole stockholders.

The initial purpose of the business was to contract with the state for the management of the prison. (The corporate purpose would be expanded greatly with "Double D" becoming the registered brand of a rich livestock enterprise, among other lucrative developments.) The personable pair bargained with the state authorities to run the prison at a per diem rate of seventy-six cents per inmate. They agreed between themselves that Driscoll, the entrepreneurial brain and the more energetic of the two, should be the warden, and Daniels would serve as business and procurement manager.

It has been said that a business partnership is a more difficult arrangement even than marriage, for if marital partners disagree they can get a divorce, but interwoven business affairs may defy separation. At any rate, Driscoll and Daniels got along very well together throughout their lifetimes to their grand mutual profit. (Which is better than Driscoll did in his personal life: some years after the formation of the Double D Corporation, his first wife ran off with a banker/politician who had been a prison trusty.)

The primitive penitentiary whose control the Double D Corporation took over was composed of a collection of log buildings situated on eleven acres at the southern edge of Cottonwood, a small but commercially important town. Its perimeter was defined and its inmates held more or less securely by a sixteen-foot-high fence of rough boards.

On the very first day of the venture, a near-escape through the gap of a loosened one-by-eight-foot fence board gave the new warden an opportunity to demonstrate with showy style that his administration was to be taken seriously.

Driscoll was an astute opportunist, but he was much, much more: he had a flair for the dramatic; his sense of timing was gifted, as was his degree of intelligence, self-assurance, skill as a marksman, and intuitive understanding of the people about him. He was a big man, standing six-foot-two and built solid like the butt end of a tamarack tree, signaling strength and physical competence not to be messed with. Yet his threatening aura of brute force was tempered somewhat by a facial expression customarily canted toward calm and good nature. A full mustache on his oval, sleepy-eyed face hid his lips like a miniature, fraying canopy, making it difficult to accurately judge his age—was he closer to twenty or thirty?

At noon on that pivotal day, having directed that the population of sixty or so inmates be assembled in four lines on the prison yard, the new warden strode before them wearing, among other things, a large sombrero, a gun belt and a leather vest. Standing hands on hips, with neither bluster nor condescension, he said matter-of-factly, "As you know, there has been a change of leadership in this penitentiary as of midnight last night. Now, sometime early this morning, someone here attempted to tinker with the surrounding fence," he gestured with a circular motion of his head, "and seemed to have in mind making a run for it. That was a foolish thing to do. Our only responsibility is to keep you here, and that, you may be sure, is what we intend to do." Motioning to the fence with his raised left hand, he continued.

"From now on, none of you, no inmate, is to go any closer than ten feet to that fence. Anyone seen in the forbidden area will be presumed to be making an attempt to escape and will be shot on the spot." In the following long moment of electric quiet, he looked challengingly into the face of each man standing before him. The effect was an unequivocal, and very personal, message.

Relaxing his intensity ever so slightly, but remaining deadly serious, the warden crooked his right index finger, summoning a trusty from one side of the inmate gathering to step before him. Into the hands of the puzzled inmate he placed an empty, quart-size, glass milk bottle, saying, "Here, Emerson, I want you to take and throw this bottle straight up in the air as high as you can. You understand?"

"Sir, you want me to take this here bottle and throw it right up in the air there," the man said, looking at the new warden questioningly, "as high as I kin?"

"That's right. You stand right over there on that bare spot, and when I say 'throw' you toss that bottle as high as you can."

On command, the bottle was thrown into the air, all eyes following it; at the same instant the warden drew a pistol from his belt, aimed it at the peak of the container's flight, then fired one blast that caused eyelids to blink and pieces of glass to fall to the earth.

To put an emphatic cap on things, the trusty was directed to select from among the fallen shards one fragment to be thrown high as a target for a second shot; that too was shattered by a bullet, whereupon the warden, holstering his gun, gestured the trusty back to his position with the others, and, addressing the captive assemblage once more, said: "I hope that makes our intentions clear." Except for a few nervous coughs and shuffling feet, a profound silence indicated that the message had been received. It is doubtful that many wardens have initially established themselves with such panache.

By the end of the Double D's first contract year, the prison population had grown to some ninety inmates, which was quite an insufficient number at seventy-six cents per head per day to provide an income satisfactory to the stockholders. Accordingly, just as thousands of other entrepreneurs in other specialties have done, the enterprising Driscoll set out to peddle his product. Off and on for several months he traveled the state, employing his untutored but winning abilities at public speaking to stump for greater emphasis on strict law enforcement. The result, as intended, was an increasing prison population. In a collateral move—which, incidentally, launched him on an important side career as a legislative lobbyist—he encouraged a bill through the legislature that required reimbursement of county sheriffs by the state for the expense of delivering convicted felons to the penitentiary. While such savings for the counties may seem modest today, they were significant in those times, and they contributed directly to an increase in the number of prison inmates.

In conjunction with his speaking forays, the warden built friendships with local lawmen and gained popularity among ordinary citizens by assisting on posses and by participating in shows of marksmanship. (Years later an old-timer recalled with feeling that Driscoll had been the very best shot in the state: "Yes sir, that fellar could shoot a rattlesnake in the eye crawlin' in bunch grass at two hunnert feet!") He seldom forgot a face or a name, an ability that endeared him to countless men grateful for a hero whom they expansively regarded as a personal friend. His popularity not only contributed to an increasing prison population, but it led to a base of political support, which would be very important in the days to come.

In these activities one sees the emerging outlines of a dynamic mix of copious self-interest and studied public purpose that was to characterize the warden's long tenure. In hindsight one sees, too, that they bespoke a lopsided personal makeup, which would finally result in the man's downfall.

Up to the time of the state's placement of penitentiary management in private hands, inmates spent their days in almost total idleness, which, coupled with the rigid imposition of silence, a common penal practice of the time, was deadly boring, personally destructive, and wasteful of human potential. Driscoll liked neither the silence nor the desultory idleness; although he fell short of being a fervent idealist, he had a capacity (here one sees another of the several conflicting sides of the man) for compassion and caring. "The first purpose of a prison is to punish," he explained to serious prison watchers, "but punishment is foolishly profligate if, when a man has done his time, he returns to the free world unchanged for the better in attitude and behavior."

Warden Driscoll began at once to innovate. He inaugurated a Morning Court where disciplinary infractions were dealt with daily and where inmates had an opportunity to talk directly with him—"The

Man"; he moderated the stultifying, hard-to-enforce silent system, permitting inmates to talk with one another at their assignments, in their cells, and about the yard. With money provided by a wealthy hunting partner, he established a marching band whose musical output was perhaps never of the highest quality, but it constructively occupied some of the time of its members and provided entertainment for others. He set up a library for inmate use. (Of this he kept very strict control, insisting that no publication could be included without his personal review and stamp of approval. He once wrote scathingly to a publishing house, accusing them of "attempting to sneak in a book" some of whose passages he considered too sexually explicit.) He took a personal interest in the affairs of many of his charges and did not hesitate to counsel and advise very directly in some instances, even to the extent of forbidding certain romantic relationships and personally reading the incoming and outgoing mail to assure compliance.

But his greatest concern was inmate idleness, and to meet the problem Driscoll moved quickly to initiate institutional work projects. The first of these, astoundingly ambitious, was a proposal to construct a granite wall three feet thick and sixteen feet tall with castle-like turrets at its corners and midpoints to replace the ridiculously insecure wooden fence. It was a massive project, denigrated by onlookers, who saw it as an impractical dream. How could a population of horse thieves, rustlers, and robbers, among whom there was not one with experience as a stone mason, build a rock wall of such proportions?

A dreamer Driscoll may have been, but impractical he was not. Under direction of the prison maintenance supervisor, to whom he gave high praise, a large crew of men was sent out daily under guard to a nearby quarry where granite blocks were cut and then hauled in on a railroad spur especially built for the project by a second crew. In less than a year, to the astonishment of the early detractors, the impossible wall stood completed, and it stands foreboding to this day.

As an incentive and reward for such work—and for much more to follow—Driscoll introduced a system of "good time," innovative for its day, by which a conscientious worker might earn a shortened length of stay.

In the meantime, the penal population was increasing significantly; crowding became the new problem. Without lament, one presumes (the recruitment program was paying off), Driscoll dealt with this eventuality by setting inmate crews to work building and operating a brickyard, whose output provided the main structural components of a cellblock with space for 200 men. Remarkably, again, it was built and put into service in less than a year's time.

As useful as these projects were in occupying the hours of idle men, they were insufficient to employ all of the inmates who were willing to work. But the warden had more imaginative projects in mind. Bounty hunting was perhaps the more novel of these.

For several years, reflective of the times and the pristine locale as well as Driscoll's own love of hunting, a small selection of exceptionally trusted inmates were allowed to go individually throughout the surrounding valley and its ancillary mountain ravines to hunt bears and coyotes. The inmate hunters collected the bounty for their kills, and the area's bear population in particular was virtually wiped out—to the gratitude of the local ranchers.

All across the valley, too, countless water wells were drilled for grateful farmers; eager inmates were mustered for snow removal in the winter and flood control in the spring; a few even carried the mail. (One of the mail carriers, unable to withstand temptation, got involved with a housewife on his route to the titillation of the entire prison population—where does news travel more quickly than through a prison grapevine? The suspicious eyes of other women along the route, impatient with the frequent tardiness of their mail, soon caught on and sent word to the warden who, on learning of the affair, personally rode out and gave the woman what for in the presence of her husband, and the straying mailman was locked away from direct sunlight for a good long time.)

Work gangs of up to seventy-five qualifying inmates were sent out to various counties across the large state where, housed in tent camps, supervised by three unarmed guards, they built hundreds of miles of public roads and numerous public buildings.

The single biggest public beneficiary of prison labor over many years, however, was the town of Cottonwood itself. Impressively, it was inmates who dug the town's main well, installed the entire city water system, built and maintained the streets. These ventures, worthy from the standpoint of inmate well-being and possible rehabilitation, coincidentally bore political and economic advantage to Driscoll and to sponsoring politicians, who had jointly arranged for the work to be done at considerable savings over regular labor.

Within a few years, as all of these developments gained credence and momentum, Driscoll was the genial recipient of national recognition for his penal programs. His views and descriptions of his innovations were sought from across the nation. He became a frequent, able, and surprisingly polished speaker invited to appear before various groups of prison administrators, lawmakers, and others. To a group of prison wardens he confidently stated:

> The correct theory of a penal institution is not founded on the relation of a vindictive master and suffering slave, but on the relation of teacher and pupil, of nurse and ward, of parent and child. In order that reformation may find foothold, a prisoner must not lose his identity. He must be encouraged to think along elevating lines and to direct his mind in channels that lead toward higher and better things. He must be allowed to still hold or gain back his self-respect.

This was in an era when inmates were expected to become penitent for their misdeeds, encouraged to humility and personal rebirth through silent contemplation, prayer, and religious worship. Driscoll made no secret of his disagreement; it was, he said, work, not prayer, religion, or idleness and silence that would salvage inmates:

> The direct effect of outdoor life, regular habits, and employment on prisoners cannot be too lightly estimated. [The inmate] works willingly and with the necessary punch and vim that accomplishes beneficial results every day. From the brow of the burglar and the bank robber drops the sweat of honest toil. They get time to reflect on the futility of their past life; their muscles are developed by steady labor. . . . The horse thief and the cattle rustler wield the pick, the axe, and the shovel as though they were to the manner born.

Driscoll was established nationally as a penologist of exceptional leadership and organizational ability. Officials of the Prison Reform League gave him glowing praise:

> [Driscoll] seems to anticipate every reform that this League desires to put in effect. . . . If we decide that a move would be of benefit to the prisoners it is generally found that it already is in force in . . . [his] penitentiary.

But such acclaim was not enough.

Sam Driscoll was far too energetic and ambitious to settle on penology as a single-track career. Smart, self-assured, strong-willed, he exercised leadership in other spheres partly from greed and partly for the glory of it; for one of his nature there was simply no other way. He was as zealous in seeking influence and economic fortune as to being in the limelight, to being needed and appreciated. He was a pragmatic, creative, and crafty man whose inner forces compelled him to take charge, to build, to improve, and to acquire.

Of considerable advantage to Sam Driscoll in his pursuit of wealth and power was an innate capacity for graciousness and charm. He was a "people person" who loved to mix, to have a good time, and to see that others enjoyed themselves too. He was often the host and guide for coveted hunting trips, which he carefully arranged, always including a trusty inmate or two to do the cooking and dishwashing. Closer to town, his home, an attractive, rambling bungalow built just across the street from the prison, was the frequent scene of generous entertainment ranging from quiet poker games to grand parties catered by inmate attendants and enjoyed by the influential and famous. Driscoll came to know them all, loved their company and they loved his; and they used each other to individual advantage in the ways of politicians, career-makers, and interlocking directorships: you scratch my back and I'll scratch yours, but never so crassly stated.

On the other hand, it should be said to the credit of his outgoing nature that no one was too insignificant to merit his friendship and generosity: he had many friends among ordinary people. Several times a year, too, residents of the wider community were invited to attend band concerts, plays, and even dances within the prison walls. These occasions were anticipated with high interest and were regarded as top social events. As such, they were duly and glowingly reported by the local paper.

Driscoll's initial success at influencing members of the legislature to vote measures benefiting the prison (and, thereby, the Double D Corporation) led directly to an extended avocation as a lobbyist. Drawing on his ever-widening friendships with the state's politicians and his alliances with the even more powerful corporate leaders who could make or break them, Driscoll became a smoothly effective and influential figure behind the scenes of law-making, where his efforts went far beyond matters of the prison or law enforcement. It became generally known among the main politicos that Driscoll was a man to know and be friends with for the sake of one's own political career. Well-financed by his clients, his lobbying entertainments were lavish, on the surface social and benign, but they had strings attached to be pulled later when a critical vote was coming up. And when ordinary guile, wining and dining, and other customary gratuities were insufficient to "persuade" a wavering legislator in a critical instance, Driscoll did not shy from boldly offering cash bribes—illegal, of course, but a practice not unheard of at the time.

In his memoirs, written long after Driscoll's death, a United States Senator respected for his honesty, after humorously telling of Driscoll's effort to bribe him, goes on to recount a backroom yarn bespeaking Driscoll's reputation for ruthlessness and appetite for money: Contrasting markedly with the quality of his penal reforms ran the quiet understanding that any big interests that wanted to get rid of someone who was an annoyance could get him shipped off to the state pen without the trouble of a court appearance and formal sentence–for a fee! Though unproved, it was a story whose telling sprang from an insiders' belief that slick payments for special favors and questionable services were a two-way street for hale fellows Driscoll and his partner Daniels and that money, in the proper amounts, got things, even illegal and outlandish things, done.

One of Driscoll's major coups–highly self-serving if not quite dishonorable–was achieved in concert with some of his powerful, carefully cultivated friends, and it had very significant political and economic ramifications. This was the persuasion of the Northwest Railroad to establish a division point with a payroll of 1,000 employees in the town of Cottonwood. The influx of that many wage earners into a town of less than 2,000 souls was pot-of-gold news to the local businesspeople, who never forgot who buttered their bread for them. The slick thing about it was that by this time the Double D Corporation stood as the community's major business enterprise, one of whose timely endeavors had become the construction and sale of family homes–using prison labor of course. (Today, still to be seen throughout Cottonwood are numerous plainly rectangular hip-roofed houses originally built by the Double D using inmate crews, with lumber from the inmate-operated Double D sawmill and chimneys made of bricks shaped by the hands of inmates and fired in the prison kiln.)

So far as the Cottonwood newspaper was concerned, Driscoll was one of the town's principal pillars, referred to in only the most approving terms. If, while other local businesspeople prospered and the prison got high marks in penal circles, Driscoll and his partner played politics and became well-to-do, the paper made no objection. The mainstream individuals of Cottonwood, seeking their own measures of wealth and power but not having Driscoll's personal gifts of initiative, leadership ability, charm, and persuasiveness had very early hitched their destinies to his. It was not mere happenstance that Driscoll served as the mayor of Cottonwood for a total of twelve terms–twenty-four years in all–and that he was unopposed in all but two elections.

Elsewhere, others had begun to wonder.

By 1909, twenty years into Driscoll's wardenship, it was a matter of record that the Double D Corporation had increased a modest farmstead, originally acquired for the production of foodstuffs and other materials for the prison, to a total of more than 10,000 acres of ranchland running herds of horses, cattle, and sheep; it also owned mining claims, water rights, two ice houses, and a lumber mill plus half of all the houses in Cottonwood. Ranches, horses, cattle, ice, sawmills, and city lots and houses were worth money, big money. Among themselves, some people were quietly asking what Driscoll and his partner, who had started out as modest wage earners, were now worth. Just what kind of money was there in the prison business? And how much of it was legitimate?

That same year, a strong governor and his advisors reached the conclusion that contracting for the prison operation had some very serious flaws and that it was time to change the arrangement. Management of the pen, they determined, should go back to direct state control. Their decision seemed based on factors so clear-cut, and the governor's determination seemed so forceful that Driscoll's growing number of critics thought that he was surely out of office. But their judgement was premature.

Driscoll's response to the governor was stridently unyielding: "If I am to be replaced as the warden, the state will first have to compensate my corporation for our investment in prison structures and come up with what you owe us for unpaid contract fees and other legal obligations."

To avoid a nasty political squabble fueled by the warden's grassroots following, the governor reluctantly agreed that Driscoll should stay on as warden, but as an appointed state employee; the contract system was terminated. And Sam Driscoll held the wardenship for fourteen more years with little or no change in pace or manner. In Cottonwood and about the state he was known as "Big Chief." He continued to make deals and do favors, some of impressive scale, like securing World War I surplus cars and trucks through eastern "friends" for every county in the state as well as the state highway department.

Meanwhile, the warden's within-the-walls construction program had continued, not at the frantic pace of the granite wall and the first cellblock, but steadily; it finally resulted in an institution in which all of the buildings, holding some 600 inmates, were recent and of the latest design. (It was in one of these that Inmate Straight had been confined.)

The last of these structures, Driscoll's greatest pride, was a 700-seat theatre, incongruously built in 1919 along the lines of the era's pretentious, movie-palace architecture and decor. The building was one conceived over several convivial evenings by Driscoll and a friend, one of the state's wealthiest, most ruthless and powerful, but sometimes sentimentally generous, magnates who, atypically in this instance, requested anonymity. The gift was sufficient to provide the necessary materials as well as the interior furnishings, drapes, seats, and stage necessities, all of which were put together by prison labor. The result was a theatre equaling any of the day in the entire state. In it weekly movies, frequent plays and concerts not only countered the barrenness of prison existence in those times before radio and TV, but presented a privilege and disciplinary tool, very simple but very helpful to prison management: misbehave and you were denied the show! Citizens of the surrounding community, too, were often invited in to enjoy an evening of free entertainment.

It has been said that power makes its own rules. There are ample historical records to show, however, that when rules are unduly skewed on behalf of their promulgator, the cumulative indiscretions lead to his or her demise.

For many years Driscoll, largely unchallenged, had made the rules of his prison fiefdom, not only for its inmates, but for its transactions with the wider world as well. And his "rules" pertaining to prison property and labor were very much set to accommodate his own interests. Inventories were loosely kept or were nonexistent. Respective properties of the prison and the Double D Corporation were often exchanged or mingled, generally to the latter's advantage. The use of prison labor went far beyond rehabilitation or an innocent alternative to idleness.

Finally, however, in 1921, after a total of thirty-four years at the prison, first briefly as a guard, and then as the man in charge, Warden Driscoll's tenure was abruptly ended. A governor of the same political party but with no obligations to him, newly elected on a hard-swinging reform platform, told Driscoll he was through and gave him a generous two weeks to clear out.

In spite of the urging of his many friends to scrap it out with the governor, Driscoll did not formally contest the action. It was unlike him to give up, but it had perhaps become clear to him that the governor now had the legal authority as well as the political power to dismiss him. But his departure, far from gracious, was characterized by acrimonious public outbursts revealing a surprising capacity for imbalanced coarseness: " . . . the Bolshevik governor has put the can on me . . . ," " . . . the puking governor has it in for me . . . ," " . . . who does that political snake think he is?" and much more. Half of the prison staff quit their jobs in support of the warden, protesting the governor's action, but to no avail. A popular state game warden (of such was the stuff of appointive qualification) was named to replace him.

The Cottonwood weekly paper took no pleasure in the governor's move; far from asking who the warden thought HE was in view of announced discrepancies of his administration, the paper claimed Driscoll's victimization and supported him heartily. The newspapers of some other towns, however, praised the governor's "courageous move" in taking the "long overdue step."

The governor did not stop with simple dismissal. After a six-month audit and special investigation (at whose close the auditors stated that some of the records were in such a hopeless muddle that it would take years, if ever, to unravel them), he brought charges of misuse and mismanagement of prison funds against the stewing ex-warden. The ensuing trial without a jury in front of a district court judge (and friend of Driscoll's) dragged on for months, the transcript of its proceedings filling 10,000 pages. At the close of it all Driscoll was found not guilty of the fifteen technical charges made against him, but he was ordered by the court to return to the prison one automobile (a black Packard, seven-passenger touring sedan—no mention made of the condition of its rear seat space), ten tires, a pipe-fitting machine, and several small objects. Far from clearing the situation, the trial's outcome only stimulated clamorous and prolonged controversy about the warden's culpability and the governor's motives in removing him.

Eighty-five days before any hint of the warden's summary dismissal, the prison theatre, which Driscoll proudly regarded as the greatest single achievement of his extended building program, was gutted by a midnight fire of mysterious and never-to-be determined origin. (Were the factors of the fire really that fragmentary? One wonders: the investigating state fire marshal was a frequent hunting partner of Driscoll's; his political appointment had been secured several years before by some of the warden's astute string-pulling). Only the concrete floor, the four masonry walls, and the colonnaded front portico remained. It was the heart-breaking loss of Driscoll's fondest prison showpiece.

In none of the extensive records and news articles relating to the prison and the affairs of Warden Driscoll or in the transcript of his trial does one find a hint, let alone proof, of an inside bootleg enterprise as related by San Quentin lifer Straight. And yet, the strangely concatenated circumstances of Driscoll's wardenship make it seem possible . . . it does just seem possible that there was a still in the back basement of the prison theatre and that a dysfunction of the apparatus (explosions of bootlegger stills were not at all uncommon during prohibition) started the fire that destroyed the warden's dream house.

Whether one accepts lifer Straight's story of the prison bootlegging enterprise as fanciful or real, the construction and then the puzzling, fiery loss of an uncharacteristically posh prison building of unusually genteel purpose ironically symbolize the splendid but seriously flawed career of an exceptional warden and his qualities of creativity, iron will, leadership, humanity, ambition . . . and greed.

Eight Weeks Waitin'

Irst thing Monday morning I received a hand-scrawled note:

> I got to see you soon as possible. Nobody in this place is doin nuthin for me. This is important. I need to see you right away.
>
> Cora Staley A-77016

Because of a large number of previous appointments and other prison duties, it was Wednesday before I could see Cora Staley. As in preparing for interviews with other inmates whom I didn't know, I checked the inmate's file out of the records office and reviewed it moments before she came to my office.

The photograph on the inside cover showed her to be a large woman—large around anyway. Her head, like a snowman's, seemed set on enormous shoulders with no neck at all. The adjustable lanyard that held her prison number on the shelf of her bosom must have been extended full-length to reach around her. Her frozen facial expression was one of dull-witted anger, but I was cautious about making character evaluations on the basis of hastily snapped, official photos. She had entered prison eight weeks ago on a conviction for welfare fraud; her previous record was one of petty theft and numerous instances of shoplifting. Clearly, she had been an exasperating public annoyance, although she seemed to present no threat of more serious crimes.

The scant review of her record had not fully prepared me for the impact of the thirty-year-old woman who came through my office door. I was astonished. She was larger, even, than I had expected, not tall, but her circumference was vast. Each step across the floor seemed to require conscious effort, like a crane operator moving a suspended wrecking ball over the ground, cautiously lifting it, easing it a few inches forward, then gently setting it down. The bulge of her breasts in a styleless cotton frock was large indeed. I briefly wondered how long a human heart could sustain such bulk.

Were it not for the dullness of her expression and a perpetual frown, her face would have been attractive. Her skin was a rich milk chocolate with paler highlights on the cheeks. Heavy black eyebrows, severely drawn together, canopied dark eyes whose flaccid expression was "I-know-you're-against-me-but-I'm-comin'-after-you-anyway," rather than one of appeal.

Here was a ponderous, blunt-minded woman whose response to the vicissitudes of life was bitterness and anger. Quite unaware of her limited ability to comprehend, she saw the world as a threatening place in which people could be trusted only to misuse and take advantage of her, a belief so concrete that it was beyond paranoia–it was the foundation of her existence. She simply *knew* that some powerful, privileged, variously favored people had beautiful, affluent lives that she sorely envied; she wanted and deserved the good things as much as they, but nobody, including God, was willing for her to have them. There was no other way for her to explain her poverty.

She ignored my greeting and my gesture to take a chair (the straight-back chair at the side of my desk–she could not possibly have settled between the arms of the one winged chair) and stood in the middle of the room a tenuous distance from me. A nervous tic flickered at the left corner of her pouting, brightly colored lips.

"I got to have some help, man. Nobody in this place cares about what happens to a person. They tell me you the onliest person in here who can help. You gotta do somethin'. They say when I come in here that staff s'pose to care about you, s'pose to help you with your troubles. Ain't nobody helped me with nothin'!"

From deep behind her angry complaints and disagreeableness one felt the presence of an unwanted child who could never have known the warmth of a mother's arms, the refuge of a mother's bosom. To sense such deprivation made the woman little less difficult to endure, however; her greatest skill seemed to be the alienation of potential friends and advocates. I quickly felt an impatience with her and her grating voice. Still, I had a responsibility to understand what she saw as her problem and to determine what could be done about it.

"All right, Cora. Please tell me what it is that you need help with."

For a moment she looked at me doubtfully. I seemed to have spoken too soon, interrupting her recitation of grievances; she appeared reluctant to turn from a self-satisfying harangue to something more specific. But, with a concentrated scowl and twitching cheek, she condescended an explicit response.

"I been in here for eight weeks. When I got here from county jail I had one raggedy brassiere. One. Tha's all I had, man. I tole 'em at the clothing room that I only had the one raggedy bra and that I had to have some more. That ugly ole white bitch in the clothing room say they didn't have no brassieres my size. She say it look like I need somethin' size of a circus tent and couldn't I furnish my own. I didn't like that what she said 'bout a circus tent; she shoulda said somethin' like that. And to furnish my own! How'm I gonna furnish my own? So that fool say they'd have to order me some, but she didn't know when they might get here. I been back to the clothing room two, three times ever' week and they ain't got them bras in yet. I don't think that old woman ever tried to get 'em. You may not can tell, but I got big ... uh ... you know ... big breasts, and I can't go around with nothin' holdin' 'em. Now I want you to get me some action, man!"

Was I hearing this correctly? Over the years I had been confronted with many inmate requests and complaints. By now, many of them fit into categories that had their own procedural responses. But this problem was unprecedented in my experience–entirely new–and it took me a moment to adjust to its novelty. At the same time I felt relieved, too, for the matter was simple and direct. If this was all she was seeking, it would not require action from the legislature, clemency from the governor, or a threat of suit by the ACLU to get results.

Simultaneously, I felt strongly displeased. If someone down the line had given a damn, this inmate's need, assuming that what she said was substantially correct, should have been taken care of long before. No matter the quality of her rhetoric or how inadequate and irascible her personal manner may have been, she should have had more responsible attention.

"Cora, you are telling me about a problem with which I have had no experience. But if you have been here already eight weeks with only one raggedy bra, I'm sure that your problem is real, and we should be doing something about it."

Cora was unmoved by my acknowledgement of her need and the official failure to deal promptly with it. She resumed her critical discourse.

"That ole clothing room lady never done nothin' for me, man. They don' care 'bout people in this place. I been eight weeks waitin'. You know how that feels in a raggedy bra?"

"Uh, no ... I don't. And I'm not here to talk about the clothing room or that 'old lady,' but I believe you when you say that you need this item of clothing. Now, please try to hold onto your anger for a minute and tell me what I need to know if I am going to be of help: how do I order a bra? Do they come in sizes?"

"Sure, man. How you think you buys 'em? You got to have a size!"

"Yes. So, for you, what size do we need to look for? That's what I need to know."

"What I need is size . . . uh . . . size 48, man."

"Okay. Size 48."

"Yeah, 48 . . . with double F cup."

"All right. Size 48, double F cup. That's all I need to know?"

"Right. I just needs size 48, double F cup. Don't forget the double F cup. Eight of 'em. I got to have eight of 'em. That gives me some for washin' and some for spares."

"All right, I've got that. This is the problem that you wanted to see me about, and this is what you want me to take care of, right?" I wanted to be sure that I had the whole story, but without encouraging her to expand the list.

"Yes. Nobody in here cares nothin' 'bout it . . . ."

"Cora," I interrupted, "here is what I am going to do: I will check with the clothing room and see if they have ordered bras for you. If they have not, then we'll see that they do so, and put a rush on it. At any rate, I promise you that, one way or another, we will have some bras for you within a week. Now will that take care of the problem?"

It would have been out of character for Cora to concede anything like courteous acknowledgement of my attention and the promised action. "A week's a long time, man. You can't do no better?"

"This is a new kind of problem for me, Ms. Staley. I don't know where or how quickly we can get these things. But I do promise you that as soon as possible, and within a week, we'll have some bras of proper size for you."

"Well, if tha's the best you can do. You better not be givin' me no runaround! I needs them bras!"

As the unseen crane operator eased Cora toward the door, I wondered how rash a promise I had made. If the clothing room were really not able to get results, my weekend recreation might have to be a trip to L.A. to hunt up the pledged apparel. "Oh well, charge it to adventure and don't lose your sense of humor—you're adding to your fund of knowledge," I told myself.

With lingering awe I watched the progress of Inmate Staley as she crossed the room, firmly setting in my mind the outlines of size 48, double F cup. At the door she placed a surprisingly dainty, brightly manicured hand on the knob, engineered a slight turn toward me, and said with marvelous disdain, "If I don' get better service than I been gettin' in this place, you don' need to think that I'm ever comin' back to this prison again!"

A Circle of Coyotes

Gary Lone Eagle was a natural leader, not because he set out to be, but because he was built that way. He was a handsome six-teen-year-old: black hair falling shiny, shoulder-long, brown eyes, skin the color of caramel, and slender body. His straight nose suggested white blood in his background, and some of his mannerisms seemed more white than stereotypically Indian: a ready smile, quick wit, and gregarious charm. Other boys followed him because of his rousing, keep-it-moving energy, natural athletic skill, and self-assurance, which put him out front and carried others along with him. He was a bright boy, capable of serious moments, but most of all he was a fun-lover—sometimes getting carried away with it—which was a reason for his presence in the juvenile training school.

When it had been proposed that a campus "cultural group" of Native American boys be formed, it was Gary who was elected "chief" with only one dissenting vote. At the first get-together of the school's seven Indian boys in Assistant Superintendent Marken's office, Gary and Wonder Morgan were the early arrivals. Gary, polite and good-natured, sat easily in a red leather conference chair, hands on his widespread, jean-clad knees, and spoke comfortably with their sponsor: "Hey, Mr. Marken! You're gonna start a club for the Indian guys, huh? Great idea. When we gonna start?"

"He's startin' it tonight, ain't you, Mr. Marken! Where's the other guys? You sent for the best guys first, huh, Mr. Marken? Well, here we are!" said Wonder Morgan as he wandered about the office, stopping to finger a small brass replica cannon that stood on one of the bookcases, clicking a radio on and off, examining family pictures on Marken's desk. "Who's this, Mr. Marken? Is this your daughter? Cool! Think she'd go out with me? You probably wouldn't let her, wouldja! Ha ha ha!"

In contrast to Gary, Wonder was taller, filling his white t-shirt a lit-tle too amply, large arms more fat than muscular, his skin showing a faintly reddish glow. Although he was eighteen years old, Wonder often had the brash and intrusive demeanor of a five- or six-year-old. His face was pleasant and he frequently smiled or chuckled nervously, but without quite making contact. His thoughts, flitting like a chickadee, were nearly always self-centered.

"What do you keep in all of those desk drawers, Mr. Marken? I'm gonna check 'em out. . . . " But just as Wonder was reaching for a drawer handle his attention was diverted by the arrival of a second pair of boys. "Hey, here's Mutt and Jeff–ha ha ha–the Dragonflys! We gonna have flies in this group, Mr. Marken? Ha ha ha."

David, the older of the Dragonfly brothers, was large-boned and overweight, big belly lopping over his leather belt; his round, full face was impassive. The younger boy, Corey, very thin and fine-featured, frequently smiling shyly, politely laughed at Wonder Morgan's tired joke. They took chairs on the far side of the room's small conference table as the office door pushed open again and three more boys hesitantly entered, checking out Marken behind his desk, then Gary and the Dragonflys. To the obvious annoyance of all, their entrance was announced by Wonder singing, "One little, two little, three little Indians–ha ha ha!" but when the others did not respond to his cheerleading gestures to join in the song he dropped into the armchair at the end of Marken's desk, briefly daunted. These three entrants were William Falling Thunder, Richard Buffalo Runner, and Terry Yellow Wolf.

The youngest of them, barely thirteen, was William Falling Thunder, for whom the main person in the whole world was Gary Lone Eagle, next to whom he dragged a chair and sat down, poking Gary on the shoulder with a loosely clenched fist, a huge smile lighting his ordinarily inscrutable face. Gary and William were from the same town in the northwest corner of the state, where they had been well-acquainted before being sent here by the juvenile court.

Richard Buffalo Runner was, in physical appearance, the classical young brave: lithe, dark-complexioned, almond-eyed with high cheekbones, his blue jeans outlining rather bowed legs. His slightly hooknosed profile might have been the boy image of the chief on the Indian nickel. He was good-natured, friendly, very bright, and so quiet that he tended to be overlooked, but it would become clear that he thought more deeply, more philosophically, than did any of the others.

Over the years Marken had seen too many Indian boys much as these come to the school, disappear into the woodwork, then, months later, "graduate" to chronic alcoholism, premature–often violent– death, or to adult prisons and mental hospitals. He had to admit that the school's staff members had–as had many Indians themselves–fallen into a defeated assumption that to be Indian meant to be forever dirt-poor and live in pockets of degradation; that it meant drunkenness or other addiction, even among the very young, and it meant hunger, neglect, abuse, and inept and caved-in families. Any consideration of "future" had long since been abandoned; a boy's life was lived for the moment in vacant-lot ballgames, summertime swimming in the river, stealing bicycles (later, cars), smoking, drinking, shoplifting, and sexual promiscuity. To be an Indian, in short, was to be a loser.

He had long been thinking that some special effort had to be made to interrupt this pattern, but what to do? The idea of starting a club had occurred to him soon after Terry Yellow Wolf, the seventh of the boys now in his office, had come to the school.

In spite of some drunken vandalism of a public school that represented an active anger at whites, Terry did not regard himself as a predestined failure as did so many. His home was in an Indian settlement, distinctly different from a city slum or a reservation. His band had purchased land, which was located on wooded hills along a meandering river only an hour's drive from the training school. The people of the settlement had their problems, their internal tribal differences and conflicts, but they had accomplishments and satisfactions as well. The adults went out into the surrounding white man's world and worked, returning home to their families and tribal ways on nights and weekends. Terry had a close-knit family, some of whom came to visit him almost every weekend. He was fluent in his native language—spoke English with an accent—and he had a remarkable knowledge of folklore, history, and the rudiments of his native religion. Very much in touch with and proud of his past, he, atypically, had a goal for his future: he intended to be a diesel caterpillar operator.

In comparison with Terry, the other boys, all city-dwellers, were only "nominal" Indians, for most of them knew little or nothing of their backgrounds. It was Marken's hope, however idealistic, that the members of a club might be put in touch with the world of their ancestors—before towns and schools and cops, before the white man—and that a justified pride in their origins might thereby be encouraged. And might not a greater sense of themselves enable some of them to reach for something fuller than the squalor, drunkenness, and ennui resulting from the collapse of a noble, "primitive" culture?

In proposing his idea to the boys present in his office, Marken kept it simple: "I've been wondering if you boys would like to have a club. It would be just for boys of Indian ancestry, nobody else. It would have two purposes: one, you could all get together for some group fun and recreation; and two, you could spend some time learning and talking about where you came from, that is, about the old Indian customs and beliefs and ways of life. Anybody interested?"

That they might have a club exclusive to Native Americans, special attention just for themselves, with one of school's main men as its sponsor, was an inviting proposition, perhaps more for the fun than the "culture."

"Cool idea! I think we should do it. When could we meet?" Others nodded in agreement with Gary Lone Eagle's bright-eyed enthusiasm.

Rousing from his pouting silence, Wonder Morgan burst in with: "Yeah, Mr. Marken, let's do it! Where would we meet?"

"We could meet one evening a week. Our main headquarters would be the volunteer center, and we could have games outdoors or go to the gym."

"How about food? Could we eat there sometimes?" It was unusual for William Falling Thunder to speak out, but he seemed to feel safe under Gary's wing.

"How come just one evening a week? Why not on weekends, too?" asked the younger Dragonfly.

"Hey, no, Mr. Marken! We should take over the volunteer center for us guys and live there! How about that, Mr. Marken?" Wonder Morgan was getting wound up.

"Don't get carried away, Wonder," Gary laughed. "Next you'll be askin' for girls to come to a dance or something!"

"Great idea! Why not, Mr. Marken? Maybe your daughter could come!"

At this Marken ducked his head and raised his arms, signaling Wonder to back off, a good-natured gesture that indicated that there were decorous limits. This put the others at ease and brought some laughter. Things were getting loosened up.

As the laughter died down, Terry Yellow Wolf, customarily taciturn, spoke out: "We should have a club. There is a lot of good stuff we can do: make handcrafts to sell, learn about religion, learn about where guys' names come from. I could get some people to come from the settlement sometimes to help." Although not as charismatic as Gary, Terry was a devoted and serious exponent of an Indian's being Indian, which placed him in a unique position of authority.

Interrupting again, Wonder flashed a new whim: "Hey, Mr. Marken, Terry's right. I want to do the fun stuff, but I want to learn about the old ways too, because someday, if I ever get out of this dump, I want to work on behalf of my people!" It was a peculiarly paradoxical comment from this hyper handful of impulsive energy. "But," thought Marken, "it's a goal. Who knows? Give it time."

It was agreed that there would be a club; its twofold purpose, as suggested, would be to have an organized, recreational "brotherhood" and to learn about Plains Indian customs, beliefs, and folkways. It was further agreed that the group would be formed on the order of a tribal secret society (interesting "fraternities" unknown to the boys but described by Marken) and be led by an elected chief, with group discussion and "business" to be conducted in council, the chief presiding.

Wonder Morgan, bouncing in his chair, shouted, "I want to be chief, I want to be chief," but the others ignored him and heartily declared Gary Lone Eagle their leader, a role into which Gary stepped easily, starting right off with, "Okay, first thing we gotta do is get a name for the club."

After many suggestions (like "Morgan's Men," from Wonder), much laughter, arguing, serious thought and discussion, the name "Coyote Society" was agreed on.

Through good fortune, an unusual opportunity arose to start the group off with an adventure that appropriately combined physical activity and cultural relevance. During some long-ago time, the area a few miles from the training school had been the location of campgrounds of unknown people of the plains. Now, in the spring of the year, when fields in these reaches were prepared for planting, shiny steel plowshares, cleaving deep into rich black soil, often turned up long-embedded arrowheads, scrapers, and an occasional stone hatchet.

A good-spirited farmer (not all neighboring farmers were so friendly to the school and its students) gave permission for the group to search his fields for such ancestral implements in the few days interval between plowing and planting. The welcome prospect held an element of mystery: a search for artifacts–"What's an artifact, Mr. Marken?"–was beyond the experience of these boys, but they were game to try.

The idea to take a group of mostly city-reared Indian boys out into the countryside and, in effect, turn them loose was viewed with headshaking disapproval by some of the staff. True, groups of training school students were taken off campus from time to time to attend recreational or entertainment events, but always with very close supervision to forestall the possible attempt by someone to run away. (Runaways were not appreciated by the surrounding citizens; they also caused staff extra, unpopular work, usually at odd hours, when every effort had to be made to catch the runner before he hurt himself or stole a car or otherwise disturbed the general peace.) Was there a risk in turning the Coyotes loose within defined, but quite extended, boundaries with only one adult watching them? What one or more of them might do with this relative freedom was indeed a question, but the outing would have to be a test of their loyalty to their new club and its future. And so, despite the wagging heads and muttered comments, the group went out.

Almost immediately on arrival at the river, William Falling Thunder, the least likely to make a find, kicking around in the dirt near the car, shouted out incredulously, "I've found something! I've found something!" And sure enough, he held in his outstretched palm half of a black, obsidian arrowhead. His was the glory of being first, probably for the first time in his life.

Gary Lone Eagle at once said, "That kid's got sharp eyes; I want him for my partner!" And William seemed three inches taller for the rest of the day. He was a lost, insecure lad who needed some successes and brotherly acclaim.

The search over 600 hilly acres divided into fields by growths of timber was on in earnest, with six of the boys pairing off and Wonder Morgan going out by himself. And when the time was up and dusk was on them, every youth, even the lethargic David Dragonfly, had found at least one verifiable fragment. Gary Lone Eagle had found three choice points, one of which he gave to William. Wonder Morgan found a perfect, very sharp point and–perhaps the best find of all–a small stone hatchet-head, and he coaxed, "Bring us back tomorrow, Mr. Marken. You're a wheel. You can do it! At least you could bring me!"

There was loud boasting about who was the more talented searcher and who had the better finds. For some, but not Terry Yellow Wolf, the traditionalist, or Richard Buffalo Runner, the thinker, the historical significance of their treasures was of lesser importance than their evidence of the finder's superior powers to search them out.

If the thought of running away had occurred to anyone it had been fleeting.

While the Coyotes had varying levels of interest and curiosity about Plains Indian culture and life-ways, it was soon obvious that their combined motivation did not quite add up to a red-skinned Boy Scout troop bent on earning merit badges for topical studies.

The most popular activities were basketball and swimming. Basketball hardly had cultural relevance, for it had no direct Plains Indian antecedent, but it is standard for American kids of all ethnic origins, and it brought about some welcome games with boys from the nearby settlement. Having learned of the Coyote Society through

Terry Yellow Wolf's family, approving adults soon arranged to take teams of settlement boys to play basketball against the Coyotes once a month in games of aggressive commitment but genial sportsmanship. They were usually accompanied by several carloads of spectators who came along to cheer for the home team. It was all in fun; the adversaries were, after all, "brothers."

Skinny-dipping, even in an indoor pool, can be related to Indian culture. Being able to swim strongly was a matter of survival for Indian males, who were expected to cleanse body and soul, first in a sweat lodge and then with a splash in the river or lake during all seasons of the year, even when ice had to be broken to gain a waterway. Swimming, too, uses up lots of energy, as Marken soon discovered in his unanticipated role as the "victim" of occasional friendly, but strenuous, in-water grappling matches entitled "drown the white man." Just who had started this event was not remembered–it could only have been Wonder or Gary–but it quickly became a hilarious near-ritual in which two or three boys (one or more of whom might otherwise be quite shy of him) would "catch" Marken in the deeper end and pile laughingly on, pushing him under, to their joy and his vigorous retaliation. An outcome was the nickname of White Man for Marken, a warm, if backhanded, expression of respect and popularity.

An occasional good-weather alternative to basketball and swimming was a Cheyenne variation of the game of tag; it required stamina but no special equipment other than plenty of outdoor space. As in any tag game, IT, the designated target, was pursued by the others, but in this case by a single file of boys, each with his hands on the waist of the boy in front of him. For the Coyotes, this resulted in a six-man line whose lead member had to reach out and tag IT, an accomplishment requiring cooperative footwork. As the centipede-like column ran around trees and across the grass there were many wipe-outs and pile-ups, bringing the glory of skinned knees and elbows, braggadocio badges to be condescendingly displayed to lessers–that is, non-Indians–on a hero's return to his dorm.

Following an hour, more or less, of such vigorous activity, the Coyotes made do with the volunteer center, a converted old farmhouse at the east edge of the campus, for a meeting place. Old-time secret society members would have fearfully shunned such a square-cornered shelter; for them the only thinkable indoor gathering place was a tepee in which no sharp corners permitted evil spirits to hide. Also, a tepee's circular base symbolized the interconnectedness of all things, a verity always to be borne in mind: was not life itself a circle starting in the Spirit World with birth and returning there at death?

Fortunately, the entrance to the center's main room, which by imaginative definition became the club's "lodge," correctly met the essential of facing the rising sun as any tepee should. And so, shoving the furniture aside, the Coyotes would settle cross-legged in a circle on the floor with Chief Gary Lone Eagle sitting at its westernmost point, properly facing the east. Subdued from an hour's workout, the others took places around to his right or left according to their status. "White Man" Marken thoughtfully took a place outside of the circle, alert to when his guidance was needed, but, as far as possible, leaving the proceedings in the hands of its exclusive membership.

A meeting was properly started when Gary pressed Bull Durham into a long, wooden-stemmed, red stone peace pipe, lighted it with a match, and passed it along the circle, each "brave" offering it to the four winds, then taking three puffs in a ritual that was always performed with a mixture of relish (it was a way to get a smoke) and surprising dignity. Gary Lone Eagle had such an infectious sense of the dramatic that the others, at first more reticent and self-conscious, became seriously engrossed in the enactment of such customs. A proper mood thus set, there would follow the reading of a folktale or a description and consideration of some old custom. Boys will be boys of course, and sometimes monkeyshines and kidding around got in the way, but usually the meetings were serious and attitudes thoughtful.

Terry Yellow Wolf was a frequent, soft-spoken, but earnest presenter. The extent of his knowledge and the depth of his conviction—no priest in a pulpit ever appeared more sincere—gripped the attention of the group. When he spoke of the Spirit World, you knew that he knew there was one.

Terry's description of the rite of the "medicine dream" evoked special and recurrent interest. The milestones between boyhood and manhood were very clear and highly spiritual in Indian culture. "An Indian boy did not become a man," Terry said, "until he had a dream in which he learned of his medicine." 'Medicine' meant a religious, sort of magical helper—usually an animal, but sometimes other objects of nature. After the elders and medicine men got a boy ready, he had to go alone to a mountaintop, where he fasted and made sacrifices—like chopping off part of a finger—for four days and nights until he slept in exhaustion and had his dream. Then he would return and the medicine man would explain what the dream meant and what the secret medicine of the boy-becoming-a-man was to be. From then on the 'helper' would be a major spiritual source of the boy's strength in life endeavors; he had earned the right to go out on the hunt, to make war, and to count coup, the bravest act of all. Terry said that even now an Indian could gain personal strength in this way if he would go to the trouble.

A great interest of almost all youngsters is food, and the Coyotes were no exception. William Falling Thunder had raised the question about food in the very first meeting, and he did not give up. "When are we gonna have something to eat or drink at these meetings, Mr. Marken?" (He never got quite brave enough to address Marken as "White Man" as did most of the others.)

Marken understood the importance of refreshments for a group, but he insisted that for the Coyotes the food should have some cultural relevance:"If you guys can think of something to eat that is typically Native American, we'll see about having it. Just remember: No secret societies that I ever heard of sat around drinking Cokes at their meetings!"

Old Indian cuisine was more utilitarian than gourmet. The daily menu of the Plains Indians was based largely on successfully hunting buffalo and lesser animals, whose meat was eaten raw, dried, roasted, or boiled with supplements of roots and berries. But berries, wild meat, and roots were foreign and unobtainable to the Coyotes.

However, Gary Lone Eagle, who was often on balance between fun and more serious endeavors, had the answer: "How about having fry bread?"

"All right! You got it, Lone Eagle!"

"Fry bread! Let's do it!"

At one time or another, each of the boys had been to a modern-day powwow, where fried bread is as regular as cotton candy is to a county fair. While the dish had probably been introduced to the Indians by whites in the first place, who could deny that fried bread had become an authentic Indian food? Some traditions have just been around longer than others. So it was agreed that the Coyote Society should have a meal, private and apart, with fried bread for basic authenticity.

The school's baker generously mixed up a batch of bread dough, albeit with enriched white flour. And the food director indulgently produced a large iron fry pan, a gallon of cooking oil, plus hamburger patties, corn (what could be more authentic for some tribes than corn, never mind that it came out of a can), lettuce, and, inevitably, soda pop. Forget that food preparation is women's work; on an electric stove in the kitchen of the volunteer center the Dragonflys and Richard Buffalo Runner deep-fried flattened gobs of dough to a golden brown, appetizing to look at, but very likely, it seemed, to challenge even the most robust of digestive systems.

The meal was prolonged and successful. The boys' capacity for food was astounding, and when it had all been eaten, no interest was shown in physical exercise. Brown bodies with distended abdomens sat or lay about the lodge. Some slept, others reminisced. It was unanimously agreed that a feast should thereafter be held once a month.

For a special meeting of a more serious nature, it was arranged for a respected settlement elder, George Big Bear, to come to the training school and talk to the club. This was a generous undertaking, as George Big Bear was old and frail. The Coyotes planned a feast to honor their guest, whose visit they anticipated with restrained excitement.

The meal, including fried bread, was served family-style at a long table, boys seated on either side. George Big Bear was placed at the head, and the two younger men who had brought him were seated at the far end. There was little conversation during the meal: the boys stoked in their food; George Big Bear nibbled at his in detachment, his thoughts seeming to be in another place and time.

When the food had disappeared, Gary Lone Eagle rose, and with uncharacteristic reserve, thanked the two men for bringing George Big Bear to the training school. "Now," he said, in language reminiscent of old-time formality, "the Coyotes will hear George Big Bear speak to them."

George Big Bear's eyelids, like tiny louvers, tautly screened gray eyes that looked out from his stag-colored, heavily lined face at one boy and another, then drifted away. His old-man voice was soft, and his words had fringes of native accent. Remaining seated, he spoke with natural dignity.

"Since I am eighty-six, my lifetime bridges the old days and the new. Now I do not have much time before I return to the Spirit World. I have had a good life. Yes, I often felt the evil of prejudice, but even so I had many pleasures in my time. My people stayed together on our own lands, not on a reservation. That way the government does not so often tell us what to do. We get along fairly well with the white man. We no longer hunt for a living, but we are still closer to the old ways than are most reservation Indians.

"Long ago, when I was still a boy, I had a dream. In it the voice of the West Wind spoke to me and said that, although I could not ignore the evil of white man's greed, which had destroyed the life of my ancestors, I should not let resentment rule my days. Anger would only destroy me; it would not change my enemies. 'The old ways were wise and good,' said the West Wind, 'and there is much in them that will serve you yet today if you will look carefully. Look to your ancestors for strength and wisdom. Be brave and proud like them!'

"My grandfather, who had been a chief in the old times, told me to listen to the dream for it was a medicine dream, very rare anymore. 'You are favored by the spirits,' he said. 'The West Wind is your medicine. You are lucky to have a helper. As the West Wind told you in the dream, pride and bravery were the two most important personal strengths of your forebears. They had to be brave to hunt wild animals for food and clothing and to fight off their enemies. And in doing those things well they held big pride.' That's what my grandfather said the dream was telling me.

"And so I learned that bravery and pride are just as important today as ever, but in a different way. Now, Indians have a right to be proud of who they are. We came from strong, noble people who respected the earth and all of nature and honored the Spirit World. No other peoples have better beginnings than we in our ancestors. Yes, we—you—can be proud. And more than ever we need to be brave—not brave for the hunt or for tribal warfare anymore, but brave to reach out and make a good life for ourselves and our families within the ways of the white man, ways that we cannot change. We all can draw on the strength of our ancestors to build a good life in our own time, for ourselves and our children."

George Big Bear sat back in silence and fatigue. He had finished speaking. His short presentation was followed by no white-man-style applause, only a deferential silence that gave no clue to the depth of the listeners' understanding.

One by one, the boys pushed back their chairs, rose, and began the clean-up, carrying dishes to the kitchen. Richard Buffalo Runner, the thoughtful one who so seldom spoke, returned and cleared the place in front of George Big Bear. "Thanks for coming to our meeting, George," he said with respectful familiarity. "I will remember your medicine dream and what the West Wind taught you." One boy, at least, had been strongly impressed by the old man's words.

On a gray Sunday morning many weeks later, a call came to Marken from Terry Yellow Wolf's uncle at the settlement. George Big Bear had died. "The funeral is this afternoon. You should bring the Coyotes." Typically austere, the message, not so adorned as an invitation, was firmly expectant—members of the group, having been briefly included in the circle of a respected elder's life, should be present for the ceremony of his death.

During the drive to the settlement, there was mutual excitement among the boys. To have an outing from the training school on the spur of the moment was an event whose novelty eclipsed regard for the passing of an old man. Still, there was something about the occasion—partly that they were wanted, and that Marken was seeing to it that they got there—that provoked restraint.

By the time of their arrival, the service was under way in the settlement church, a white frame building with a weathered wooden cross at the peak of its green metal roof. Stepping from the midst of six or eight adults who stood in silence on the lean-to porch, Terry's uncle motioned the boys up the wooden steps and through the double doors into the plain, amber-windowed sanctuary. Moving awkwardly, large-eyed, unsure of themselves, the boys squeezed into seats here and there among stony-faced Indian women in dark shawls and men in woolen mackinaws. Beneath the altar painting of a crucified Indian Jesus, a young white preacher was conducting a Christian service of kind words, standard hymns, and the Lord's Prayer. After the benediction, six tribal elders bore the plain pine coffin out from the church to a shiny Buick hearse, then followed on foot as the vehicle crawled along the wide trail to the isolation of the tribal burial place.

Hunching into the mist, the mourners, a hundred or so, took a narrower back-trail some little distance to the top of the wooded knoll where stubby, grayed boards among the dripping trees marked random graves. There they gathered round a freshly dug hole in the rocky ground; close by rested the opened casket embracing the body of George Big Bear, clad in his fringed and beaded buckskin coat and leggings, the eagle feathers of his headdress stirring slightly in a light breeze.

A near-blind, bareheaded old man, face framed by waist-length gray braids, stepped to the foot of the casket and spoke rapidly for some moments in the tribal tongue. Extending his palms waist high, turning his body alternately, he said his last words to the ground, to the sky, and to the four points of the compass, acknowledging the Spirit World whence they had all come and to which their friend was now returning at the close of his life's circle; gently nodding, he gestured the end of the spoken ceremony.

One by one, the somber mourners filed by the casket placing gifts beside the body—food, a knife, beaded moccasins, gloves, and other essentials for the spirit journey along the Hanging Road from earth to heaven. Unobtrusively guided by Terry's uncle, the Coyotes melded in, each dropping a pinch of tobacco in the casket and moving on, wordlessly taking another trail down through the woods with the others to the council hall and the ceremonial feast.

After several weeks of regular, ordinary sessions, an unforgettable society meeting quite unexpectedly occurred.

Following a noisy and tiring hour of water polo, Gary Lone Eagle, unusually serious and business-like, convened the Coyotes with the opening ritual of the peace pipe and then announced, "I have a special project for tonight. What we will do is: each guy will take a turn at lying down in the center of the circle as though he's dead and in an open coffin. Then, the other guys–the surviving guys–will have a funeral for him. Each in turn will stand over the playing-dead one and say some last words for him. Okay?"

Just where Gary had come by this solemn plan he did not say and no one asked, but the hushed response of all but one was, "Hey, yeah, let's try that!"

Terry Yellow Wolf was reluctant. "I will watch from outside the circle," he said, "but I don't want to pretend to be dead, and I don't want to speak over someone else as if he had died. No. That might make something bad happen. I don't want to tempt any of the spirits to do something bad."

Torn between the novelty of the proceedings and the caution raised by Terry, no one was quite comfortable to be first in the role of newly departed or of eulogizer. But Gary spoke encouragingly, saying that no one had to do it unless he wanted to.

Smiling gamely, always anxious to win Gary's approval, William Falling Thunder stepped self-consciously to the center of the circle, lay down on his back on the soft carpet, brown belly showing at the gap between blue jeans and white t-shirt, and folded his hands on his chest much as the body of George Big Bear had lain in its coffin.

Somberly, Gary took a position above William's head and spoke with touching impact. "William was my younger almost-brother, the closest to a brother that I had. Who could ever have had a more loyal friend than him? He was a generous kid who never hurt anybody, always willing to share whatever he had. William was too young to die; the spirits ended the circle of his life too soon. Now he is gone before ever having learned to believe in himself or how important he was to other people."

The Dragonfly brothers in turn spoke next. David, the older one, though not openly negative, usually showed little vitality. For William, however, he spoke out with extraordinary feeling and a degree of commitment that was surprising. "William was a really good kid. He was always generous and friendly, and he was loyal to his friends, especially to Gary. He had a really tough young life–tougher than most Indian kids; he didn't even know who his mom and dad were, but maybe he will meet them now in the Spirit World."

Corey Dragonfly echoed his brother with expressions of honor and sorrow that seemed genuinely felt and convincing.

From the various speakers, William Falling Thunder heard more of his worth and of his importance to others than he had heard in all of his thirteen years, and, the brief speeches for him concluded, he moved back to a place in the circle with glistening eyes and a pathetically grateful smile.

Similarly touching eulogies were offered–by Indian boys often thought to be frivolous, shallow, and uncaring–for Wonder Morgan, Richard Buffalo Runner, and David and Corey Dragonfly.

Gary Lone Eagle was the last to lie down as the one departed. For him, William Falling Thunder, his face drawn and sober and wet with tears, was the first to speak.

"Gary was my big brother. He always shared stuff with me and protected me from bigger guys. He saved my life once back home when I was drunk and fell through the ice on the river. He risked his own life to pull me out when some other guys just stood and laughed. When Gary got sent to the training school I went and got caught doin' somethin' bad so I could get sent here too. I guess Gary is my big medicine. I don't know why the spirits had to take him. . . . " There was a catch in the boy's throat; fresh teardrops ran down his smooth cheeks as he barely whispered, "I don't think I can make it without you, Gary."

Other faces around the circle were now wet, too.

Wonder Morgan, the constant clown and mischievous agitator, was the final speaker. Could he accept the pervasive sadness or would he flippantly deny it? Taking his position above Gary, Wonder's taut face was gray, the corners of his mouth turned down. Earnestly, looking directly at no one, he spoke.

"Sometimes I hated you, Gary. You were a better athlete than me. You were smarter than me in school. You were better looking than I am; girls always liked you better. I hated you for that. I feel bad that I felt that way, Gary. If it hadn't been for you this club would never be. You looked out for yourself, but you thought of us other guys too. You could make things happen, not just for yourself, but for all of us. Sometimes I was not nice to you, but you never held it against me. You always included me in. I know that you like me even though sometimes . . . sometimes I wonder how anybody likes me." The boy's statement was as much a revelation to himself as it was a testimony to Gary.

Streaming tears dripping from Wonder's chin spotted his blue corduroy shirt as he continued: "Gary, I'm sorry that sometimes I was bad to you. We guys can't . . . let you be dead. Gary . . . "

Unable to say more, Wonder twisted away and sank to the floor; clutching his head to his knees, he sobbed openly.

All of a sudden, Gary, unable to maintain his immobile death-position, covered his face with his hands and, very much alive, rolled over onto his stomach, his body shaking. What he had started as "pretend," had become far more than acting. Everyone—even Terry Yellow Wolf outside of the circle—was now weeping uncontrollably. Each of these sometimes-delinquent, happy-go-lucky Indian hearts had fallen to the ground, every boy caught up in emotion so intense that it left no room for embarrassment.

Taken quite by surprise—the event's independent introduction by Gary Lone Eagle, Terry Yellow Wolf's expressed fear of it, the degree of commitment of each boy to his role, and the depth of the resulting emotion—Marken sat in wonder, greatly moved himself. He had never seen such an outpouring of sentiment from a group of boys of any racial background.

Several minutes passed.

Finally, Gary, turning on his side and raising up slowly from the waist, braced himself on one elbow. Awkwardly pulling a white handkerchief from his hip pocket, he dried his eyes, then handed the cloth to Wonder Morgan, who blotted his own face and passed the damp wad to William Falling Thunder.

Looking around at the others with a wistful, what-has-come-about? half-smile, Gary said, "I guess we didn't know what big medicine the thought of death can be."

Instead of a regular meeting the following week, the group, back in rough-and-tumble form, went into town to see the movie *Little Big Man*. Wonder Morgan had sighted the title on the theater schedule weeks before, and the group had seconded his suggestion that attendance was essential for the Coyotes. It was a movie about Indians, wasn't it?

In the van on the way to the theatre, Wonder was in peak form, glowing in the success of having promoted the movie and, as always, pushing for more—more action, more freedom, more indulgence of one sort or another.

"Hey, White Man," he called from the rear seat, "you're gonna buy us popcorn and soda, ain't you? We'll take the large sizes! What's a movie without treats, man? If I had the money I'd buy treats for everyone—even you, White Man! But no money! So you're buyin', ain't you, White Man?"

"Somewhere, not too deep inside of you, Wonder Redskin," responded Marken, "there is something like a white brat that never lets up!"

The others laughed loudly. They were often cautiously awed by Wonder's audacity, but they also enjoyed it when he got a good-natured whack in return.

The Coyotes thumped down the sloping aisle of the ornate, aging theatre and filed into a row on the left side of the house just as the lights dimmed and previews of coming attractions began showing on the screen. There was confusion as coats were removed and seats were settled into–not an easy adjustment with a container of soda in one hand and a cardboard bucket of popcorn in the other.

The movie had lots of action, lots of Indians, and much detail drawn from Indian life, including the Sun Dance, which, for some tribes, was the supreme expression of their religion. In this mystical ritual, a medicine man inserted pegs of wood through two pairs of vertical cuts in the muscles of a brave's chest, making two H's, and attached the ends of the pegs to thongs that extended far out from the center pole of a large, ceremonial shelter. Pulling against these leathers the brave danced until, hours later, the pegs tore excruciatingly through slowly severing flesh, freeing the worshipper from the attachments and ensuring the fulfillment of his vows.

The boys were absorbed in the drama, occasionally shouting, "All right!" . . . "Oh, no!" . . . "Cool!"

There was little chatter on the way back to the school, everyone seeming tired and ready for bed. Even Wonder, the irrepressible, said only, "That was cool the way that one guy scalped that white guy."

And William Falling Thunder said, "I could never do the Sun Dance and tear them sticks out of my chest like that."

As the van pulled up to its last stop in front of Richard Buffalo Runner's dormitory, Marken was surprised to hear this quiet boy speak. And what he said with unmistakable conviction was astonishing: "I'm glad that I wasn't an old-time Indian. That was too hard a life." Adding, "Thanks for the show," he was out of the van and up the walk. His usual silence did not mean that he was not involved. More than any other, he was the boy who pondered things. Surely he had for months been mulling the life-ways of his ancestors. It was he who had thanked George Big Bear for sharing his modern medicine dream. Perhaps Richard had said it to himself before, but tonight he had said it aloud: a modern way of living was more attractive to him than were the rigorous ways of the past.

Richard Buffalo Runner's words hung long in Marken's mind. Did they mean, he wondered, that Richard was searching out a way to make a niche for himself in the white man's world? Could he draw on prideful reserves of ancestral accomplishment to carry him into something other than a ghetto existence in his future? And, would the white world let him achieve a niche in view of whom he so obviously was and where he'd come from?

It was not long after that the Coyote Society disbanded—folded, really —with as little ceremony as it had begun.

The training school staff was often under unfortunate pressure to make room for the constant influx of new commitments by releasing boys before they or their families were considered to be ready. Because of this, Gary Lone Eagle, who had been there the longest, was paroled. In the next few weeks the other Coyotes were released too, joyous in their anticipation of freedom to go their separate ways.

David and Corey Dragonfly went to another state to live with their mother, about whom not a great deal was known.

Terry Yellow Wolf returned to the settlement, where he went back to school. Some years later word came that he was an over-the-road truck driver. Not quite the diesel cat operator he'd dreamt of being, but close.

Wonder Morgan reached the age of nineteen, which made him an adult in the eyes of the law. (Quite a contrast to the old-time measure of a man.) It also meant that he received a direct discharge from the school. It was not long until he somehow made his way to a reservation where an activist Indian organization was attempting a takeover of tribal affairs, demanding concessions from the government and political autonomy for the tribe. From there, Wonder occasionally telephoned Marken in the middle of the night on the one outgoing line.

"Hello, White Man? Know who this is?"

"Of course I know, Redskin!"

"I'm here helping fight the pigs, man!"

"Where is 'here,' Redskin?"

"Wounded Knee. Where else?"

"Oh, right. Who are the pigs?"

"They're the FBI, man. They're all around here. They are probably bugging this call. Now they'll have your name on their list—ha ha! It's a stand-off now, but we'll get rid of 'em and get justice for my people."

Since leaving the school, Wonder had picked up some political concepts. The clown had become a revolutionary. Though now legally a man with a romantic concern for "his people," he was still a needy little boy in many ways, anxious for acceptance and approval—in quantities of the "large size."

Gary Lone Eagle, too, phoned from time to time. "Just callin' to say hello. Heard from any of the guys?" He was a fun-seeker, not a revolutionary. When he phoned there often seemed to be a party going on in the background.

Friends at the settlement said that Gary had shown up there a couple of times–hitchhiked clear across the state to visit, especially to see a girl he had met at George Big Bear's funeral feast. They were glad to see him smiling his warming smile, cracking jokes. His bubbling nature made people feel good. On the quiet, though, they said that they were afraid he was drinking and partying too much–not when he was at the settlement, but from things he told them, at home. It didn't sound too good.

After several months of no news, Marken was roused from bed to accept a collect call at 4:30 in the morning.

"Hello. This is Gary."

"Yes, I thought so. You all right?"

"I'm all right–sorta scared."

"Scared? How come?"

"Been havin' a party. It's over now. They just took one of the guys to the hospital. My uncle. Two years older'n me. We hadda fight. Me'n him. I busted him a good one. I wish I hadn't. He's my uncle. They said they think he'll be all right. I don't even know what we was fightin' about. I'm sorta scared. What if he don't make it? But they said he'll prob'ly be all right."

"Your voice sounds like you got busted too."

"Naw. I'm all right. My mouth's full. I'm eatin' a hamburger."

Weeks later, Marken answered his telephone, waiting while dime after dime chimed into a pay phone somewhere. As if from out of a cave came the sound of a woman's voice.

"Hello. This is Gary's mother. Gary Lone Eagle. Can you come to the funeral?"

"Funeral? What funeral?" Marken asked, going weak inside.

"Uh, you don't know? Gary's funeral."

"Oh God. No . . . No, I don't know."

"Yeah. Gary. His uncle stabbed him. He's dead. It's Gary's funeral."

"No . . . not Gary . . . he can't . . . "

"Yeah," she said. "Gary. His uncle killed him. They was drinkin' two nights ago. You come to the funeral? It's tomorrow mornin'."

"Tomorrow morning. Yes . . . yes, I'll be there."

"Yes," she said softly, "you come . . . "

Could Terry Yellow Wolf have been correct in fearing that a "death meeting" would tempt the spirits to do something bad? Almost certainly, Terry would think so. Even if one held such thinking to be too primitive, still, the fear expressed had been strangely prophetic.

Five weeks after Gary's funeral, William Falling Thunder hanged himself. They found his body in the woodshed behind the shed of a house where he lived with a varying mixture of relatives and others who came and went not far from Gary Lone Eagle's place. The coroner said the boy's body had been hanging there, unnoticed and unmissed, for at least two days.

Had not that lost, looking-for-a-brother boy said, "Gary's my big medicine; I don't think I can make it without him?"

After he left the school, there was never a word of Richard Buffalo Runner. One wonders about that handsome youth who had so thoughtfully compared the rigors of the old ways with modern life and who had listened so carefully as George Big Bear told about the West Wind's message of Indian pride and bravery. But he is not one who is likely to call.

Uneasy Piece

Being big has its advantages. At six foot four and 240 pounds, I don't get hassled much in bars from creeps who want to show how tough they are; I get waited on pretty good in stores and at the service station. Also, I'm able to work a few nights a week and on weekends as a stevedore on the waterfront to earn some extra dough. With a wife and three kids—another on the way that the doc says may be a pair—it's not easy makin' it on just a state parole officer's salary. Janet and I are close. We agree that we want kids and that until ours are grown, she's the den-mother and I'm the family breadwinner. So I work two jobs, one of them requiring muscles.

People have funny ideas about bigness. Because I can "lift bales and tote barges" they take for granted that I'm tough, fearless, and invincible and like to mix it up. I've never backed down from a fight—haven't had that many, really—and have never started one myself. Actually, I'm no good with my dukes; you never saw anybody so clumsy. And as a wrestler I'd make one hell of a bear rug: if I can get you down and lie on you, I'll smother you to death! Really, I'm a whole lot better with my mouth than with my body.

One thing, I'm good at getting jobs for parolees. My size has something to do with that—I get in to see personnel directors easier than little guys do. People sort of like to be friendly with big guys. So, on the basis of that, I talk my way in to a lot of places, then talk man-to-man about givin' an ex-con—murderer, robber, whatever—a job and score a pretty good percentage. Placements are always in demand, and when I have extras I share them with other guys in the office.

When it comes right down to it, you know, I'm pretty enthused about my job. That is, I believe in what I'm doing. With the right breaks some cons are going to make it, change the direction of their lives. You never know for sure which ones. So you do your best to start 'em all off pretty equal with a decent job and a place to live if they don't already have one. I never talk do-gooder lingo to a potential employer, but my do-gooder enthusiasm comes through, and a lot of people can accept that easier from a big guy who they figure couldn't possibly be a wimp than from a scrawny jerk making humanitarian pleas.

But the point I'm getting to is that, while big is good in some ways, it also has a down side. Before I get into that, though, I should tell you a little bit about our office, which is the St. Ignatius District Parole Office. There are seven of us officers in this district: two blacks, one Jew, three nondescript Caucasians, including me (I'm Danish) and our supervisor, who is second-generation Chinese and my best friend—our families get together a lot. The St. Ignatius District is known throughout the department as having the tightest bunch of guys and also the best professional record in the state. We scrap and carry on amongst ourselves, but when there's work to do or a crisis at hand we're a solid team. You can mess with us all you want, but we hang together.

And we do practical jokes like you wouldn't believe. Nothing is sacred. Nothing. I don't know how our secretaries stand it. Sometimes we embarrass the hell out of them. But they're with us 100 percent: even Lucy, who is a lush and to make it through the day has to have a nip about every half hour or so from the bottle in her desk that she thinks no one knows about. (Her bottle is about the one personal thing that nobody has ever messed with.) We make racial slurs, belittle one another's work, ridicule personal traits—it's seldom dull.

I have to admit that I'm the biggest practical joker in the bunch, and when I really burn somebody I laugh so hard that the flimsy office partitions shake, and Kati, my tiny secretary, pretends to cower, God love her. I know that sometimes I get carried away when I'm in a good mood. When I'm happy everybody's supposed to be happy! Then when I have a bad day, like being hung over after a night of heavy drinking, I go the other way and my glum mood kind of pervades the place.

Like I said, Peter Wing, the man in charge of the office, is of Oriental ancestry. I guess you would say he is typically Chinese—slender as a sixteen-penny nail but as tough as a railroad spike. Tough in character, I mean. I have no idea how tough he is physically. I don't know anybody who ever got through the armor of his wit and brains to find out about his muscles. He's as aggressive with his mouth as any of the rest of us, and usually he gets in the last word, not by pulling his rank, but just from sheer, scrappy intelligence. He's usually right in there with all of the malarkey, but once in a while something can hit him and his face takes on the flat, drawn-shade expression proverbially called 'inscrutable' when describing an Oriental. Like once when we were kidding around I called him "chinky chinky Chinaman," and the fun stopped right there. The look he shot me ground me up and fed me to the fish right there on the spot. I tried to joke him out of it, but he had drawn the boundary of what he'd put up with, and our friendship was closed down for the rest of the day. The degree of his sensitivity took me a little by surprise, and I felt sort of awkward–bad, really–about it.

Still, I don't know whether it's arrogance or stubbornness or what, but I'm not given to making verbal apologies when I've screwed up. Actually, such a prissy formality in this case would probably have separated us further and put a long-term cap on things. What I did was, next morning early, I stepped into Peter's office with raised eyebrows and big, exaggerated, is-it-safe-to-come-in eyes, pursed my lips like some prim clubwoman and said, "Would Mr. Wing care to join me for breakfast?" He drilled me with a withering stare for a second, then allowed a moderating light in his dark brown eyes, looked down at the papers on his desk, a half-smile creeping up one side of his pale face and said, "You buyin'?"

That meant he'd cooled down and we were getting back on track, and so I moved in with, "Yeah, I'm buyin'. If you order fried rice!" which brought an exaggerated frown, but then his smile widened and he stood up without looking at me, reached for his suitcoat–he dresses real good–from the coat tree in the corner and said, "Just don't take me to one of your Copenhagen fish joints."

At Curley's Diner, where we usually had one or two parolees work-ing in the back (that way we could log breakfast time as a field visit), Wing ordered the $6 breakfast steak to my mock dismay, and our joust was over, although he did complain that the steak could have been more tender.

As a supervisor Wing is the best in the business. He knows the strengths of each of us. As long as we get our reports in on time–fodder for the maw of the bureaucracy–he cuts us a lot of slack. He doesn't flaunt his authority, but of course we know it's there and un-derstand the responsibility that he carries. Peter would never be called a bleeding heart, but from the personal experience of growing up as a minority kid in the back end of a family restaurant he knows the blunt edge of injustice, and he's determined that parole services be performed with concern and responsibility–to all parties involved.

Though the system doesn't require him to, Wing carries a small caseload of selected parolees–not just easy cases–to keep his hand in the "real work" of the agency. Nobody ever mentions the fact much–compliments are never direct in this locker-room society, you under-stand–but it brings him a lot of quiet respect. Toward parolees he's always courteous, strictly matter-of-fact, and utterly fair. Make an honest effort and he's with you; screw up and you're dead. Actually, we all are pretty strict so far as that goes.

Wing guides the work of the office with a reverse kind of humor and control; that is, instead of handing out direct praise he feigns criticism or sarcasm, which might seem pretty rude to an outsider, but we all understand it and it makes us a tighter group. For example, one of our officers, Dick Spencer, is totally conscientious and hard-working. So one afternoon Wing said to him, "Damn it, Spencer, how come you've been getting in late every morning? You haven't been in before ten any day this week. Riding the gravy train again, huh?" And everybody, especially Spencer, knew that he'd just got a stroke, special recognition for putting in some very late hours—a lot more than he'd ever get paid for—in order to keep up with some challenging cases that could best be looked after at night. Naturally, he'd come in later in the morning after working until midnight.

Another time Wing might say, "Hey, Marky," (it's always Marky, never Mark) "why have you been hangin' around the office all week? Why don't you get off your fat butt and get out in the field and find out what your screw-ups are doing?" knowing full well that Mark, who is a top fieldman but hates paperwork, had been drudging away to bring his case summaries up to date.

And Mark would come back with, "Up yours, Mr. Wing, sir. Stay on my case and I'll be forced to go over your head and tell the chief about the .38 in your desk drawer!"

"You'd never do it. You're just damn glad I've got that gun in there because you think I'd come to your rescue if one of your gentile goof-ups came in here after your balls. Anyway, I'm glad to see that you're finally getting caught up on your paperwork. I just hope you're dictating it in language that the girls can understand. And keep it clean; they have sensitive ears."

Through such open banter, most service topics are dealt with in a pretty cool way; the inevitable, interpersonal sharp edges get rubbed off acceptably, and everybody knows where he stands. It's understood, furthermore, that none of the team secrets go out of the office. For instance, like what Mark said about the pistol. We all know that Wing keeps a pistol in his desk, thereby bordering on violation of departmental regulation number 37, which clearly states that an officer is forbidden to carry weapons. In Wing's hands the gun would never be misused, and everyone's glad for the subtle support that it represents. Testy incidents do sometimes occur in the office and, should one of these grow violent, though none ever had, the officers know that their supervisor would be on hand to take persuasive control.

Once in a while someone, usually me, will try to con Peter into letting him take the gun out on what looks like might be a nasty situation, but Wing always holds the line: "Parole officers carry no guns. We go by the book, and whether you like it or not, the book is unequivocal on the subject."

The department's position is that officers would be safer in the long run if it was generally known that they carry no weapons. The regulation is one that some officers–the majority, I guess–believe in, but a smaller bunch don't, and I've seen arguments go on most all night about it, between field officers that is–not between field officers and the top brass in central office.

Funny thing. Wing really is kind of a gun freak; he likes guns, spends money on them, and he doesn't like the departmental policy on weapons. There are times when I know he'd rather take a gun with him, but so long as the policy is there he is sworn to uphold it.

I'm no gun nut, don't even own one, but there are times when I think I should. As a matter of fact, more than once, when Wing was out or on vacation, I've quietly "borrowed" his piece when I had to make a pick-up by myself that I thought could be hairy. I've never told Wing about those times, which may not be quite the way to deal with one's best friend, but in this case what he doesn't know can't get him– or me–into trouble.

Anyway, in lieu of a gun, when we think a situation in the field might be dangerous we usually try to pair up. And that gets me back to what I was talking about: the good and bad of being big. I seem to be in more frequent demand for the buddy system than anyone else. Because I'm strong and fill up a doorway like a grudging gorilla, it is assumed–at least hoped–that any miscreant will collapse into ready submission at the sight of me. Or, if worse comes to worst, it is expected that I will simply take control of a man of average size by means of a one-arm bear hug, snapping ribs and crushing vertebrae. What people don't really understand is that even though a guy may look like the corner bastion of a frontier fortress, there are times when he may feel like jelly inside.

I've made my share of arrests, but when I do my hands always tremble. Getting the handcuffs on some joker takes real concentration, so I don't fumble the maneuver. I don't advertise these facts, but that's the way it is. This doesn't mean that I've ever shirked responsibility or ducked tough situations. I haven't. I'll bitch my head off before going out, but I wrestle my fear and get on with the job even though I have some personal struggles with self-confidence in situations that could be physical. Big guys, you see, aren't supposed to feel that way, and everybody thinks we're cool. I've got news for you.

One Monday morning after a long weekend–Friday had been a holiday for Columbus or somebody–I got to work on time, but I was in bad shape. The day before I had been called to work on the waterfront and I'd put in twelve hours at double pay. Not bad money. So when some of us finished up and left the docks we stopped for a beer. One beer led to another and then to boilermakers. To make a long story short, I got about two hours sleep and I was hung way over and feeling mighty irritable. After nights like that I was always mad at myself, and to do penance I'd force my mind and body to work double-hard, totally relentless.

I grumbled my way in past Kati, who gave me a knowing smile and left me be, and went straight back to my office, where I shed my coat, loosened my tie, which was pretty sloppy anyway, and hunkered at the desk. My self-imposed assignment was to dictate a summary on every one of thirty-five cases; by the day's end that would bring my papers up-to-date, and it would keep Kati busy typing for a week. As I was tinkering with my dictaphone and spreading my field sheets out on the desk, the sound of Peter's voice on the telephone came from down the hall, vaguely penetrating the fog in my head. Throbbingly, I became aware that one of his cases had screwed up over the holiday–dismal way to start a week, Peter. But that was his problem, not mine.

I closed Wing and his case troubles out of my mind, but just after I did he appeared in my doorway. "Torben," he said, then he stopped, gave me a double-take, and, grinning in recognition of my lousy condition, said, "Oh boy, do you look bad! Hey, I've got the perfect cure for you. The vice squad just called. Willie Jones has screwed up. He's been dealing drugs, heavy stuff–they've got confirmation–and maybe he's been involved in some bank robberies. We've got to check out his apartment and bring him in if he's there. Come on old buddy, it's you and me on this one. Me and Willie will fix your head right up! I'm happy to be able to offer you such a splendid cure for what ails you!"

The name Willie Jones rattled through my head like an overturned dumpster spilling empty beer cans. "You're pretty glib with the word 'we,' Wing." I took my face in my hands for a minute, willing myself above the painful pollution in my eye sockets.

I knew Willie Jones. God, did I know him! I didn't need anything to do with him today. I had had him on parole once myself and violated him on a technical; not exactly a model citizen. I had hauled him back to the joint, and our parting at the front gate wasn't what you'd call cordial. Then, when he came out again after a year or so, I'd conned Wing into supervising him so I didn't have to. He's a total loser who never worked at anything honest in his life. He loves the streetlife, big cars, and cool chicks. He's not big, not much bigger than Wing, but he's muscled like a Greek god. Violence is not his thing ordinarily, but he'd never shrink from it if pushed or cornered. He'd been busted at least once, I knew, for carrying concealed weapons, and there was an attempted murder rap on his sheet. You bet I knew the dude. I figured he would not meekly surrender to us when we showed up on his doorstep. Why did Wing have to hit me with this today? And take so much pleasure in doing it.

Not that I'd ever let Wing go out on a call like this alone. I wouldn't do that. If he had to go, I'd be the one to go with him, but I'd rub his nose in it for a while first.

"Damn it, Wing, why can't you motivate your clients to live law-abiding lives? I had that guy started on the straight and narrow. Now, because you couldn't keep a finger on the crook, you want me to go out with you and risk my life to bring him in. Whenever you get a tough one you come running to me to protect your butt. Do your own dirty work."

"Oh, listen to our great Viking god. What's the matter with you, Torben, besides a little hangover? Did your wife lock you out again this weekend? Not that I'd blame her. Hey, look man, I'm giving you a chance to be a hero, to be of great service to mankind. Against my better judgement I'll take you along and give you the inside scoop on how to apprehend a big-time violator in a truly professional way! You might even get a commendation from the governor."

"You're full of it, Wing. You've let the vice squad talk you into picking up Willie Jones so they don't have to risk their butts and you want me to go along to save your neck. If you're too chicken to go after him alone, why don't you take that shiny .38 you've got in your desk? Then when you get there, if you find that you can't handle the situation, just ask Willie to call me on the phone and I'll be right over."

"Nice try, Torben. The big shots say we're safer without guns. And if you were to take a gun, you'd probably be so nervous that you'd point it the wrong way or shoot yourself in the foot!"

We kept up the mock argument for a little while like that, insulting each other, taking time, really, to get psyched up to head out. We both knew that we were going out together, and we each had some un-spoken apprehension about the assignment, but it was going to be done. Secretly I sort of admired Wing's courage in heading out un-armed, but I also thought that it was foolish. Frankly, I had some real fear of Willie Jones, especially if we sprang a trap on him.

By now three or four other officers were around, and of course they couldn't stay out of the deal. They gathered about in the passageway or shouted from their semiscreened office spaces, laughing and prodding me and Wing on. Especially me.

"Go with him, Andersen. The state will provide you a decent burial and even look after your wife and kids if you don't come back."

"Want us to call vice and tell 'em to send a back-up 'cause you're hung over today, Torben?"

"Don't worry about Willie Jones, Torben. I've heard that he really likes you ever since you took him back to the joint. Says you set him straight. He'll be glad to see you again!"

"Okay, assholes! Quiet! I don't see any of you flakes volunteering to help your leader." When I let it all out my voice really rumbles the place, and so they sort of backed down, not sure whether I was really mad or what. "So once more I must go forth and salvage the honor of the St. Ignatius District Office for you screw-ups." I was laying on the long-suffering bit.

Wing was still smiling, but we had goofed around long enough, and it was time to go. As he headed for the front door I was oddly struck by how sharp he looked–perfectly tied tie, neat blue gabardine suit, black shoes shined. No matter what I paid for a suit I always looked like I'd slept in it, which this morning wasn't too far from right. We had to look like a weird pair. I got out of my chair and reached for my jacket; every move was a sacrificial effort. As he got to the front door, Wing called back for me to get my ass in gear: "Come on, you coward. I'll bring the car around while you get the lead out. Don't forget to bring your handcuffs–if you think you can remember how to use them!"

Pulling one arm, then the other, into my coat–my coordination was terrible–I stepped quickly into Peter's empty office, walked behind his desk, and quietly pulled open the top left-hand drawer, taking out the Walther .38 that lay there and slipping it into my inside breast pocket. My legs felt like bread dough, but I could feel the give of the floor as I moved along the cheaply carpeted hall, hurrying to catch up with Wing.

Wing and I both know the neighborhood well where Willie's apartment was located at 1767 Chestnut Street. It's a decaying district of once really elegant Victorian homes now mostly converted to apartments. We parked the similarly aging, unmarked, state Chevrolet a few doors from 1767 on the wide, one-way street and just sat checking things out for a while, keeping an eye on the ornate, stained-glass, double-door entrance at the top of the worn, gray limestone steps.

There was little movement in the street. An occasional beer truck rolled by, heading out from the warehouse in the next block. A few older men and women walked slowly along the sidewalk, greeting one another with careworn dignity, pretending to be oblivious of us but almost certainly aware that we had something to do with the law. People in these neighborhoods know the score.

There was just nothing going on and that was fine with me. The longer we sat the better. No one left or entered the house. After maybe forty-five minutes, Wing sighed and said, "Well, nothing's happening out here so we might as well go in. If Willie's there, he's probably still in bed after a big weekend. Maybe he'll have some gorgeous broad with him."

"Always hoping to cop a free look, aren't you, Peter," I said as we got out of the car.

"Can you think of something better to do?" he smarted back.

You should know by now, that's the way we get along. When we get serious there is apt to be trouble afoot.

As we walked toward the entrance, I focused hard on the carved stone lions' heads at either side of the steps, holding back a sudden wave of nausea that I blamed on my hangover, but it was probably a mixture of that and fear.

Inside the double doors, the parquet-floored foyer was worn and bare but still surprisingly handsome, surrounded by thickly varnished, beveled-wood wall paneling that spoke of affluent times long gone. Our footsteps on the spindle-railed oak staircase echoed like a Gestapo nightmare, and by the time we reached the top anyone in the house surely knew there were visitors on hand.

Floor three had obviously been for the servants; the hallway was narrow and the woodwork plain. Three doors ranged along the dim corridor. Wing went directly to the one marked "8" with an incongruously fine brass numeral, trying the door as he knocked. No response. The door was locked. Several more knocks and a call, "Willie? Willie?" yielded only silence.

"We'll go in," said Wing.

That was my cue: sometimes I double as a battering ram. We'd made similar entries before, but not at this location. I grasped the doorknob with my right hand, leaned my left shoulder against one of the two long inset panels and, with the brute force for which I am so famous and in such demand, I sprung splintering pine into the room.

Reaching through, I twisted the inside knob, and the door swung into a surprisingly spacious living room decorated right out of Esquire, or maybe Playboy. On the marble mantle of the fireplace, straight across from the door, were three dark wooden carvings of

African origin, elongated dancing figures with their backs to a mirror that went clear up to the high ceiling. To the left hung a zebra skin with unsettling, astigmatic black and white stripes. Overstuffed art deco chairs and two or three couches, accented by shiny chrome lamps and a glass-topped coffee table, filled the room expensively. Soft underfoot, a green, thick, springy carpet showing the tracks of recent vacuuming contrasted richly with the white fabric-upholstered furniture. Near the zebra skin, a columned archway opened into a dining-kitchen area with more costly white-iron-and-glass furniture. On the right side of the room, an old-fashioned, raised-panel door, painted off-white to match the richly papered walls, stood ajar. Moving left, Wing indicated with a nod that he'd check the kitchen.

I gave the paneled door a cautious push and eased a look into a huge bedroom. Sweat was running down my back, and my hands were shaking. Before crossing the threshold–I was certain someone was in there, waiting to nail me–I put my right hand to the gun in my left breast pocket. The silence was eerie and threatening. I guess I took in the whole room at a glance, but what first really registered was the biggest bed I'd ever seen, all covered with a satiny purple spread and a small fortune in sexy pillows like out of Arabian nights. Yeah, I'd bet there were some far-out nights in this place! Check the mirrored ceiling. Everything was in meticulous order. Willie had help with the housekeeping, that was for sure.

A door into the bathroom was near the corner of the room on my left, but I went first to the closet at the right. Still awkwardly clutching the gun in my pocket, I made a powerful sweep with my left arm, dragging all of the clothing from the rod to the floor in a tangle. Whoever was waiting to get me was not hiding in the closet, so I stepped around the bed and kicked the bathroom door open. No one in there either. Spell that relief; this was shaking out pretty well from the standpoint of our safety.

I allowed myself a brief moment to wonder at the opulence of the room. Like the bedroom, the bathroom ceiling–plus the walls–was covered with mirrors. The floor was deep with soft, white shag, and the finely designed, dolphin-like spouts were gold. Not brass: gold. This remodel-job had cost somebody a bundle. No question: Willie was into drugs. He wasn't footing this kind of expense on welfare or even laborer's wages.

Back at the side of the bed I peeled back the floor-length spread, leaned way over, bracing myself with one hand on the bed and the other on the floor to keep my balance, and took a look to make sure nobody was underneath. No warm bodies there, so I relaxed a little more. Unfortunately, we were not going to catch our man on this morning's raid. But the room still had to be shaken down for contraband as Wing was probably doing in the kitchen.

Janet always tells me that I'm about as delicate around the house as a bulldozer in a rose garden. Well, here it didn't matter too much. I pulled everything out of the closet with both hands and checked for secret panels, rummaged through all of the boxes and the boots and shoes, but there was nothing. I stuffed it all back in and forced the door shut with my shoulder, being careful not to splinter another panel, until the latch clicked closed. Next, I checked out everything in the white and gold-leaf dresser and matching chest of drawers, some sort of French style. I took down all of the pictures and stacked them on the floor in front of the closet door, carefully scoping the frames as I went. I pawed through all of the bookshelves and gilded drawers of the bed's headboard and finally turned up one gaudy, bejeweled, gold cigarette case in which there were some folded papers containing a white powder, not enough for major sales, but if a controlled substance, enough to bust a parolee. I probed every pillow, rolled back each of the blankets and silk sheets, felt all around the satin cover, but there was nothing more.

After going through a similar routine in the bathroom, all there was left to check was under the bed. To do that I had to lie down flat on my stomach on the soft carpet—felt sort of good. Turning my head away from the bed to get a maximum reach, I eased my right arm under and, close to the edge, my hand bumped something metal that slid away. Groping around, I located it again, and I didn't need to see it to know that it was a small gun. That gave my adrenalin another shot. Parolees are not allowed to have firearms, and this one had to belong to Willie. Had he been here . . . Oh well, no need thinking about what might have happened. Regardless of what was in the cigarette case, this gun on the premises was enough to bust our man.

Without getting up, I called, "Hey, Wing, Wing! I've found something—a gun! Come in here, I've found a gun! This guy's got a gun!"

Wing was right there, calling out as he came from the kitchen, where he had been poking around just as I was, "What's up? You find a gun?" Then, as he stepped into the bedroom, he exploded: "Andersen. What are you doing lying there on the floor? I thought you found something!"

"Back off, Wing. There's a gun under here. I told you we had to be careful with this joker. Give me a chance to get up." Raising up on my left hand and then on my knees one at a time, sliding my right hand palm-down from beneath the bed, Wing and I both got a glimpse of the gun, shiny between my fingers, at the same instant. Which was way too late because by then I was in trouble, big trouble.

"Let me see what you've found!" he said in an I-don't-believe-what-I-think-I'm-seeing tone of voice. Still in a crouch, I raised my right arm over my head and extended the gun to him, fighting a feeling of total humiliation.

"You idiot, Torben! This is my Walther! How did my Walther get in here?"

Then he immediately understood, the dawn of awareness flashing across his face. "You brought my gun with you! Is this supposed to be a joke? What the hell's going on here?"

I slumped back to the floor like a beached walrus. It was now too-damn-late clear that my breast pocket was empty and that my sensational find was Wing's pistol. Yes, indeed, it was a sensation. It had to have fallen out the first time I leaned over to take a look under the bed. I'd been so hyped up or hung over or both that I hadn't heard it hit the springy carpet and bounce out of sight. And then I'd gone on to pawing through stuff, tearing things apart all over the room with both hands and completely forgotten about it, never missed it. I'd trapped myself good.

I wailed a high-pitched laugh, which I hoped would rekindle Wing's good nature, but knowing it wouldn't. I'd really blown it, but there was no way that I was going to compromise my stubborn pride and admit error or defeat right then. Between Wing and me it was always attack, attack, attack; chew, chew, chew.

I moved into a sickening-sweet offensive, attempting a good-old-buddy con job. "Yes, Wing, it's your gun! You know how spooked you get on stake-outs."

I should have just shut up, but with overstated, condescending reasonability I went on, "I brought it along to bail you out if we got into trouble. You know Willie is a tough dude, Peter. He could just as well have been here ready to blow your head off."

"Torben, cut the crap. I can't believe you're this stupid. I would have been safer to come here by myself. Wouldn't central office go into spasms if they heard about this one!"

By now I was on my feet, still a mock supplicant. "Peter, Peter! What are you saying? I was here to protect you, maybe to save your life! Where is your gratitude?" But I was only getting myself in deeper.

Peter was not going to be charmed or joked or reasoned out of this. His Oriental face was tautly noncommittal except for his dark eyes, which bore a withering Kung Fu fury. I'd seen that intensity in him only one time before–chinky, chinky, China . . . That time I'd really hurt him. This time I guess he felt I'd double-crossed him or let him down or . . . hell, I don't know what was going through his head! All I know is that I really did look pretty stupid.

Wing eyed the small pistol, which he held with continuing disbelief, then, turning away, he slipped it into his own inner breast pocket, walked out through the living room and down the stairs without another word.

If I was still hung over I couldn't feel it now. What I felt like was a wet sail hanging limp with no breeze. Defensively, I suppose, I started getting mad at Wing for getting mad at me. I was distressed, real unhappy, but you know, it was not for having brought the gun; it was for having been so unforgivably clumsy with it.

Allow me that much, Wing, I thought.

Absently, I brushed green lint from my gray suit–not that the suit looked like much at this point–then went into the living room and, in a makeshift way, replaced the busted panel in the door, pulled it closed, and headed down the stairs, cussing myself on every step for being so awkward. Christ, Janet's always right–she said it right: I'm like a bulldozer in a rose garden.

I got down between the two stone lions on the front stoop just in time to see Peter drive off in the old gray Chevy. I didn't believe it. "He'll just drive around a couple of blocks then swing back, wheeling up to the curb in a fake gesture of running me down," I thought. Attempted manslaughter would be a natural first move toward reconciliation.

But he didn't come back around the block. He was gone.

I cooled it at the curb for ten minutes or so like I was a wheel waiting for my driver to come and pick me up, knowing well that I didn't look like anyone who had a driver. It took that long for it to soak into my head that the little dink had really left me behind. In the meantime the street had got busier, and I was feeling conspicuous among all of the black faces.

So I had two choices: catch a cab, of which there weren't many to be seen around here, or take a forty-five-minute walk back to the office. Even if I could find a taxi there was no way I was going to pay cab fare; I'd blown too much money the night before. So I headed out. Penance was coming in bigger doses today than I'd planned.

I wouldn't say it out loud to anybody, but I was hoping to myself– praying hard–as I hiked the sidewalks, then turned east toward downtown along the railroad tracks, that when I got back to the office the guys would really get on my case. Usually I don't take razzing too graciously, but on this day silence would be a whole lot worse. If, when I walked in, there was only silence, everybody avoiding me, sitting at their desks, heads down in feigned preoccupation with paperwork, it would mean that Wing had been too pissed to tell anybody any details of what had happened on the great, Torben-assisted raid of the Willie Jones apartment. It would mean that he'd come in looking like the Chinese navy at battle stations and gone straight to his office, in whose doorway there was no need for a KEEP OUT sign. Everybody would be all clammed up wondering what gives and taking no chances on making matters worse.

One thing seemed pretty clear: I'd better lay low and be Mr. Humble. The next move had to be up to Wing. No kidding, no jokes, no smart cracks from me just now. Which was not my usual way, but I'd better damn well work at it.

I'd seen Peter upset before, but never this angry. It could be a rotten few days before we got back to insulting each other again. . . .

Unacceptably Flawed

What becomes of boys and girls after they leave juvenile training schools and their few ensuing months on parole is usually unknown. The American population is remarkably mobile; like other people, the clients of a correctional system move about, and once released from oversight, there is really no way to know what becomes of them. Unlike the graduates of high schools and universities, who often continue sentimental ties with their educational roots, training school students, with rare exceptions, have no desire to acknowledge that chapter of their lives or to maintain an even intermittent liaison with its officers. Training schools do not engender alumni associations.

One delightful, albeit slow-to-arrive and tentative exception, was Billy Hockaday.

As do many regular public high schools, Midwest Training School for Boys subscribed with a national agency for the presentation by traveling speakers and performers of a series of assembly programs for its students during the course of a school year. One of these presentations that came to the school late one fall was a group of naked-to-the-waist, high-moccasined Hopi dancers wearing bright headbands of yellow, red, or purple. Indian music and dances usually are not notably engrossing, at least for long, and so for a school program, it was essential that the group's narrator sustain the interest of the audience.

On this occasion, the first to appear on the small stage of the school's aging chapel-auditorium was a white man who introduced himself as Billy Hockaday, the master of ceremonies. He was pushing the far side of middle age, but jauntily so, standing his just-average, wiry height erectly on a footing of well-polished, high-heeled boots and wearing a fringed buckskin jacket and a huge, brown ten-gallon hat.

With a touch of cockiness, skillful wit, very funny stories, and an infectious smile, he subtly but quite acceptably aligned himself with the boys of the audience, almost as if he were one of them, and soon had them warmed up and in his hands. By means of his excellent showmanship and fast repartee, he kept the basically educational performance flowing and alive. The forty-minute show had a serious message concerning respect for cultural differences and for another's religion, but it was kept lively by the words of Hockaday and some unlikely clowning by two or three of the stony-faced dancers themselves. The climax of the presentation turned solemn and moving as a traditional rain dance of great religious significance to the Hopi people was demonstrated, complete with live rattlesnakes carried about the necks of the dancers. The young audience was impressed.

As the auditorium cleared of students, now smiling and relaxed, and the dancers packed their snakes and other "props" into their waiting bus, Hockaday sought out the school's superintendent, not only as a business courtesy on behalf of the booking agency, but in the hope of satisfying a personal interest in the institution and its special purpose, a curiosity welcomed by Superintendent Fowler.

Sitting together in the latter's office, a quick rapport, deeper than mere courtesy, quickly arose between the two men. With many questions Hockaday showed a warm regard for the school's purpose: How many boys do you have here? Two hundred? Really? How long do they stay? Are most of them seriously 'bad' or are they apt to be here as runaways or orphans? Do their parents care about them? How can you do anything with a boy if you can't do something with his parents? Do you use corporal punishment when a kid misbehaves? Tell me, wasn't this school famous for a marching band that it had at one time?

Superintendent Fowler found his guest's energy so vital and his interest so sensitively appropriate that he suggested they take a brief tour of the campus and have a look around.

"I would like that very much," said Hockaday. "Our next performance is not until this evening, and it's only sixty miles down the road, so I've got some time to see whatever you care to show me."

The day had grown muggy-warm, and the shade of huge, old elm trees was welcome as the two men walked about the richly green, park-like, surprisingly open campus. Around a large oval drive stood a number of plain, flat-roofed, two-story, red brick dormitory buildings and at the far end, a school building and a gymnasium. Unique among them, standing some distance removed, was an aging, three-story, yellow and white structure, elaborately Victorian, which drew Hockaday's attention. "That ornate old building over there beyond the bend of the road looks like a museum piece. What is it used for?"

"Ah, yes. That building is no longer in use, but it has a special story. It was worn out and condemned long ago and will someday be torn down. You asked about the band that the school once had. That old building was the dormitory, very fine for its day, built for the members of the famous brass band. To be housed there was an honor, or at least, the boys who lived there had privileges that the other students didn't have."

"But you no longer have a band?" Hockaday asked with guarded surprise.

"No, there has been no band for many years–long before my time here."

Superintendent Fowler went on to explain that the training school had indeed once been well-known for its superior marching band. The handsomely uniformed organization performed on the school commons every summer Sunday, and people came from miles around by buggy, auto, and train to picnic and be entertained. Youth bands were less common in those days, and so the training school ensemble was in frequent demand for performances at fairs, parades, and other public functions, including one presidential inauguration in Washington, D.C.

While the drill and discipline involved in the band's success were held by its sponsors to be significant reformative influences on its members, there were also subtle political factors supporting its existence. The school was dependent on the state legislature for its financial support. What better way to demonstrate to legislators and their constituents the school's concern and success with delinquents than a marching band of neatly scrubbed, polished, and uniformed youths whose precise drills and martial music were stirring indeed? Ah, now there was a school that was doing good things with bad boys!

For the band members, however, there had been a catch to this. When a boy qualified to be a member he could expect to be at the school for a long time. That was how band quality was maintained; good players didn't get turned loose. Band members had some compensations, privileges that ordinary students did not have: their own dormitory with more space and more liberal rules, special food, trips away from campus, and favorable attention. For some, particularly orphans or those from impoverished homes, it could be a better living than one might otherwise have on the "outs" in those days. Still, it was quite a regimented life.

But now, Superintendent Fowler said, there was no longer a band. Perhaps the instructor had retired or died. Or perhaps the rising number of commitments to the school forced such a rapid turnover of students that it was impossible to maintain a successful band. He was not sure. "Whatever the reason, by now all that remains of the band are a few photographs, some tarnished instruments in the storeroom attic, the occasional reminiscences of an old-timer, and of course, that vacant building you see there. Times change."

As Fowler spoke, Hockaday seemed to be only half-listening, absorbed in his own thoughts and engrossed with the appearance of the ornate but crumbling band cottage. Pointing a thumb over his shoulder to the old building, Hockaday turned to the superintendent and said, "You know, I . . . ," but then he shook his head; his voice seemed to choke a bit and trail off, but many visitors became sentimental on seeing lock-ups for kids. He turned away, saying simply, "Those old walls sure could tell some stories, couldn't they . . . "

As the men moved on, Fowler explained with a hint of pride that instead of a band, a monthly magazine was now the school's principal public relations instrument. "It's printed in color and produced by the vocational journalism and printing classes, whose instructors are as demanding and perfectionistic as the old band director no doubt used to be. We mail out several hundred copies every month to a list that includes state executive officials, members of the legislature, a few influential or charitable citizens, and of course copies are given to the staff and students. It's called *The Echo*, and it carries stories about institutional classes and projects, sporting events, features on staff members and individual boys, as well as short stories, poems, and cartoons. It's good for kids to see their pictures and names in print–I guess we all like that. And the teachers are careful to see that, within the state, the little magazine brings a maximum of credit and a minimum of disapproval to the school."

Hockaday picked up on the topic at once. "For years I've owned a small print shop. Could we take a quick look at your printing program? I'd like to see how you are equipped. And then I must join my dancers and be on my way."

What Hockaday saw was a surprisingly modern and complete plant with a Linotype (this was before word processors), various presses, a folding machine, and fonts of type. By chance, the current month's *Echo* had just been finished and stood in bundles on a freight dolly ready for distribution. Handing the visitor a loose copy, the superintendent called one of the students over and asked him to add Hockaday's name to the mailing list.

Many weeks later, by which time the program of the Hopi dancers and their sprightly leader were all but forgotten, the superintendent received a handwritten letter from William W. Hockaday, Hopi Land, Mesa, Arizona.

Dear Supt. Fowler:

Please forgive me for writing so belatedly to thank you for your courtesy and hospitality when I was on your campus with my Hopi dancers as a program of the Educational Features, Inc. I enjoyed talking with you and touring the school more than you could know. I thank you also for so thoughtfully placing my name on your "Echo" mailing list. I have received two issues of the little magazine and have enjoyed reading it. Your staff and boys are to be congratulated. It is very well done.

In the last issue I was especially interested in the story about the Coyote Society that you have started for your Indian boys. As you know, I have spent much of my life working on behalf of the Hopi Indians, and I applaud the efforts of your staff to lead your Indian students to a closer connection with their ancestry and to take steps to meet their heartbreaking needs in a hostile world. Don't expect immediate success. You will not be able to reach them all, but to even make the effort is commendable, and all too unusual. If I may be of any assistance please call on me. Congratulations and best wishes.

The complimentary letter was a pleasant surprise; but a postscript appearing after Billy Hockaday's signature was stunning indeed:

P.S. To be there at the training school was quite an experience for me as it was the first time I had been back since having spent four years of my boyhood there. Standing on the stage of your auditorium, seeing all of those young faces, I wanted to say to all of you that I had been a kid there once myself. And then when you so kindly took me around the campus after the performance, I almost told you as we stood looking at the band cottage—my old "home"—but I was unable to admit it. Now, stirred by the knowledge of your good work and my own sense of guilt for not having let the boys see a "successful graduate," I am taking the coward's way of telling you. And now you know!

Again, thank you for your kindness to me.

In the meager old records stored in the musty basement fileroom of the adminstration building, the superintendents's secretary found that a William W. Hockaday had indeed been committed to the school in the year 1906 at the age of fifteen as "wayward and incorrigible"; he had not been discharged until almost four years later. Her boss, she was sure, would be interested to know that the boy's birthday was

January 18th, which happened to be just five days from the day on which the extraordinary letter had been received.

Delighted with his secretary's findings, the superintendent promptly got off a birthday card with a handwritten note whose salutation read jocosely, "Dear Prodigal Son William W. Hockaday!" The note went on to thank Hockaday for his very special letter and especially for sharing the information of his "residency" at the school in his youth. "Yes, I wish that you could have told our students and our staff members too that you were once a boy here. It would have meant a great deal to all of them to see such a successful graduate. And we would have given you quite a little celebration!" This letter, in turn, brought an exuberant return-mail response of pleasure and appreciation. And that was the start of a frequent and sizeable exchange of letters and small gifts between the two until Billy Hockaday's death several years later.

Initially, Hockaday wrote mainly of his interest in the Indian club. "You must keep in mind," he said, "that most of your Indian boys, coming as they do from towns, probably know a lot more about being delinquent than about being Indian. They may know very little about their native culture and you must be patient with them. Don't expect many of them to be avid scholars."

Another time he wrote, "I think that you are on the right track when you keep your Coyotes active even if all of the games they play are not strictly Indian. I am sending you a package of small Hopi silver and turquoise trinkets to be used as special prizes for games and contests. This way, they can compete for a reward that can be related to one tribe of their people. You never know when a spark of interest will be fanned."

Then, "It is essential that Indian boys learn of their roots; without that knowledge they have nothing much that is worthy to build on. Stay at it; stay at it," he urged.

From time to time, he offered suggestions of activities that he thought especially appropriate for the Coyote Society. One of the more dramatic of these arrived by airmail late in the spring. Carefully packed in a large carton came twenty-four individually wrapped ears of naturally bright, varicolored Indian corn. "This," wrote Hockaday, "can provide the Coyotes with a money-making project. They should plant the corn at once, harvest it in the fall, and sell the decorative ears to the townspeople for table decorations. The way the Hopis plant this corn is to bore a hole the length of one's arm in the ground, drop in three or four kernels, add two mouthfuls of water, fill the hole up with dirt and leave the rest to the Great Spirit."

To plant corn that deep was unheard of by the school's farm instructor. He was skeptical; how could it ever come up? Accordingly, he helped the Coyotes plant the seeds in the rich, black soil at various depths, including arm's length, in marked consecutive plots. To everyone's surprise, all of the seeds grew, tender shoots appearing regardless of the seed depth, and with the generous rains of the region, growing lush and sweet-smelling. Hockaday was kept informed of its progress.

Plans were made for the boys to have a booth and sell the corn at the county fair. The project ended in odd failure, however. On the night before the eager harvesters were to pick their crop, a gathering of raccoons moved in and totally stripped the field of its succulent yield. Not one ear remained. The Indian boys accepted the loss with a wordless stoicism that was sad to see; none of their particular plains ancestors, they said, had been corn raisers anyway.

It was not until after many months of the letter exchange that Hockaday wrote:

I haven't told you much about my background. It is only natural, I suppose, that you might wonder why I was shipped off to the training school as a boy. I want you to know that I wasn't sent there for a serious or terrible crime! I guess that no kid thinks that he belongs there and that is sure the way I felt–still do! I have to say that I did get some good out of being there. I learned the printer's trade and I learned to play the clarinet although that was a mixed blessing. You see, I got to be too good at the music. I had to stay there a year and a half longer than most kids just because the director wouldn't let me out of the band! Oh, you bet I know all about that old band cottage that you and I saw!

With good humor, Fowler responded at once that he was surely glad to know that Billy Hockaday had not been some terrible menace or juvenile desperado.

Boiled down, the story was that Billy had a stepfather whom he strongly disliked and about whom even to this day he could say nothing good. The stepfather apparently had little or no affection for the boy, certainly no patience with him, and often beat the lad in anger. (Even now a part of the aging man's charm was a touch of flamboyance and a certain feistiness behind which one could imagine a mouthy, active, handful of a kid, not depredatory, but just in and out of things.) The boy frequently ran away from home. On one of those jaunts he was missing for several months until finally found out west living with the Hopis. That episode resulted not only in a severe beating from his stepfather but a commitment to the Midwest Training School for Boys by the juvenile court.

Billy was very bright and excelled in learning the printing trade as well as the clarinet. He enjoyed the band and was good enough to be in several small specialty groups that appealed to his love of the spotlight and were enlivened by his natural clowning ability, but his music and inherent showmanship did result in his being held at the school for a long time. So far as is known–Billy never said–he had posed no particular disciplinary problems except perhaps some occasional mouthiness. He was small for his age and often had to survive by outsmarting the bigger aggressors among his fellow students. It was undoubtedly the recollection of such experiences that had affected the man on seeing his old dormitory, but of which he had not been able to speak on the afternoon when he and Superintendent Fowler walked about the campus.

When finally released from the school to his parents, Billy had taken off within a week and returned to Arizona and his friends the Hopis, a move accepted then as good riddance so far as the stepfather was concerned.

Near Mesa, he had in time acquired land, set up a kind of trading post that dealt in Indian crafts, and later included a print shop. These small businesses became his main sources of income, although he engaged in many other sidelines such as the high school assembly circuit. Avocationally, he continued his interest in music, founding and leading several local groups; ultimately he composed the libretto for an opera with an Indian theme, a score of which is now in the training school library. It is known from a printed program of the performance that still exists that the opera was once presented in New York City.

From between the lines of his letters and the many clippings and photographs that Hockaday sent, one picked up interesting details of his life of which he did not speak directly. For instance, he had been—maybe still was–quite a ladies man. He had been married, but just how many times was not clear. He had no children of his own, but had raised several adoptive Hopi youngsters. Though he profited from trade with the Hopis, his interest in them seemed largely unselfish and of idealistic motivation. The other main theme of his life was the Masonic lodge and its charitable adjunct, the Shriners, in both of which he had held many offices and received many honors. For a time he had combined the two interests by taking his Hopi dancers about the country performing for local lodges and conventions.

Finally, well along in their friendship, Superintendent Fowler wrote to Hockaday, "Having now survived your 'confession' of a training school episode in your lurid past, would you agree to having *The Echo* do a story about you?"

Hockaday agreed–seemed quite excited about it–and sent a small avalanche of pictures: himself in a ten-gallon hat, in a Shriner's fez, in a World War I uniform with his arm around his attractive mother, himself with a group of Hopis at an honorary kiva that they had built for him, and many clippings about his work with the Hopis, the Masons, and other good works. Quite humanly, but perhaps somewhat more than most, Hockaday hungered to have his accomplishments and generous deeds known.

He expressly asked that the story tell of his appearance with a group of Hopi snake dancers on the steps of the U.S. Capitol during a drought in 1926, an event that he copiously confirmed with copies of news accounts and even the *Congressional Record*. Within two hours of the ceremony the streets of Washington had been awash in rainwater! For the Hopis the performance was a great success, not because of the rain–that was taken for granted–but because the presentation had dissuaded Congress from passing a pending act outlawing the snake dance as "pagan." The Indians were so appreciative of Hockaday's interest and sponsorship that, although they had long before made him a brave and then a chief of the tribe, they now built him a sacred kiva on his own property and dedicated it to him. No other white man had been so honored.

When the story about him appeared in *The Echo*, Hockaday was very pleased with it and sent a turquoise pendant as a gift of appreciation to its delighted author.

There was only one possible encore. After several invitations, Bill Hockaday agreed to come for a visit as a guest of the school. (His age was beginning to show: shaky handwriting, repetitive stories, and other lapses of memory.) In urging him to come, Fowler wrote, "We can offer you no honorary degrees beyond 'Boy Emeritus' [but how many people had ever been so honored?], and we cannot begin to match such a tribute as the sacred kiva given you by your Hopi friends; rather, we will put you to work performing yet more service. We want you to meet with the Coyote Society, address the student body, and give a pep talk to the staff."

Hockaday had never flown, was afraid of airplanes, and he could not bring himself to fly now. "But I will drive, I will come by car, and on the way I'll attend the national Shrine convention in Kansas City– kill two birds with one stone."

Fowler felt some concern about the aging man's taking on such a long drive. Also, some time earlier Hockaday had written that, because of a small traffic accident in which his car had knocked over a fire hydrant, his driver's license had been taken away from him. To Fowler's query, "Are you sure it's okay for you to drive?" Hockaday responded, with perhaps a trace of enduring "delinquency," that "I won't let that little accident stop me; no judge would jail an old man who wanted to make a last visit 'home' just because he didn't have a driver's license! I'm going to make it back to my 'alma mater!'"

But the trip was not meant to be. On his first morning out, Hockaday phoned Fowler quite upset. Only a few miles from Mesa, his car had blown a tire and swerved into a ditch. He was unhurt and there was no serious damage to the car, but his Indian friends, whom he had called to come help him, were telling him that this was a bad omen; he should not be going away now. "My friends have a way of knowing about such things," he said, "and so I am going out to the reservation to stay with them for a while. I am very disappointed not to be able to come visit you. Thank you, thank you for asking me and for the trouble that you have gone to."

Whether the accident had been an omen or not, the Hopis, concerned about their friend, had probably known what was best for him and stated it in the most convincing and irrefutable way.

Thereafter, the frequency of correspondence tapered off. Hockaday wrote that he was spending all available time and energy writing his memoirs–at least he was working on them when his Indians would leave him alone. They were always after him to help with some problem or other and seemed to think he was going to live forever. "As soon as I get my best seller finished, I will be writing to you!"

One more letter came from Hopi Land. Very brief, it was signed "Sadie Mathews," and it accompanied yet another gift, an attractively bound book, *Behind the Scenes in Hopi Land*, by William W. Hockaday.

Printing of the book had not been completed until after the death of the author, wrote Mathews, but he had left instructions to her that copies be sent to a list of friends, one of whom was the superintendent of the Midwest Training School for Boys. "I suppose he knew you in his lodge work," she wrote. "He had so many good friends all over the country in the Masons."

"Now who is Sadie Mathews?" wondered Fowler. Her name had not come up before. "She does not seem to know of the significance of Midwest Training School in the life of Billy Hockaday. Anyway," he thought, "she is seeing to the final affairs of a special man; let her think simply that Billy and I were Masonic brothers as she suggests."

With a mixture of pleasure at the old man's success in completing his writing and sadness that a colorful friendship had come to an end, Fowler took up the book.

Though nicely printed, it was a bit of a hodgepodge. There were many pages of photographs and reproductions of news clippings, nearly all of which Fowler had already seen. In addition, there were letters of affectionate testimony from Shrine officials, an Arizona governor, and a U.S. senator. There was a chapter on the Hopi alphabet and pictures of other benefactors of the Hopi people. A small photo, one that Fowler had not seen before, showed the Hopis dancing for rain before a massive crowd on the steps of the U.S. Capitol. That remarkable occasion must surely have been one of Billy Hockaday's finest moments.

Fowler turned to the chapter on Billy's boyhood, curious to read what the accomplished man had written of his "delinquency" and years in a state training school. What he found was touching, not for what it said, but for what it did not say.

Speaking of his youth, Hockaday wrote of his love for his "beautiful mother," who had died while he was away at World War I, and of severe beatings at the hands of his stepfather, which had led him to run away to the Hopis. He spoke of enjoying music and of happily playing the clarinet in a marching band and of learning the printer's trade in a very early vocational class. But there was no mention of nearly four years spent at the Midwest Training School for Boys.

Although Billy Hockaday, through his friendship with Superintendent Fowler, had been able to reestablish a generous and constructive contact with the site of a deeply painful, embarrassing, and somehow unrelenting event of his adolescence, he could not, before the end, share word of those four long-ago years with the acquaintances of his later, wider world; he could not believe that he might be loved the more for it. Even with all of his friendships, his successes and honors, his gifts and kindnesses to so many others, some firmly fixed fear had endured within him right to the end that, were it known that he had been a resident of a state training school for boys, he would be unforgiven, rejected ... regarded as unacceptably flawed.

Chance Encounter

A kindly curiosity about the lives and circumstances of others was a part of Kelly's nature. Wherever he went, he was alert to the people around him. On a surprising number of occasions this characteristic contributed to an unplanned encounter with someone from his past–from his hometown, school, naval service–someplace along the line. Once, in a passageway on the USS Enterprise, he quite literally ran into a former roommate, one of 6,000 servicemen being returned from the war in the Pacific. Another time at a highway rest stop in Nebraska he chanced into the man who had been his high school basketball coach years before in a town a thousand miles away. These are but two examples; it happened often.

Kelly came to regard such happenstance meetings as his own special kind of lottery, which he "won" with regularity and enjoyed immensely. His recall of names at such times did not always match his memory for faces, but his recollection of other personal details was often remarkable.

As one might expect, the likelihood of meeting once-knowns ran full-tilt when Kelly and his wife returned for summer vacation each year to the community where they had been born, raised, and spent their early adulthood. It was gratifying–warmly settling–to be among the old landmarks, taking note of the inevitable changes in both the people and the establishments of the town.

Occasionally during these homecomings, he would recognize in a lined face a child whom he had once known years before when he was a juvenile court official. Had that once rebellious, challenging, yet sometimes winning whirlwind of unpredictable, adolescent energy now really matured to the ordinary calmness, even carewornness, of middling adulthood? From time to time a tentative "do-you-remember-me?" smile from one of these might lead to a handshake or an embrace of brief reunion yielding hearty, shared reminiscences of what the two of them had survived together–or in spite of one another–in the younger one's growing-up years.

"Oh, yes. Since I last saw you, Mr. Kelly, I grew up and stayed out of trouble. Wasn't easy! I can't believe how I acted then and what a bad time I gave you. Thanks for stickin' with me. I've got three kids of my own now. I'm lucky: they're not as stupid as I was," or, "You'd be proud of me now. . . . " Words like that; mini-success stories the more warming because they represented the turnaround of reckless "prodigal sons." These were good encounters.

There were others whom Kelly similarly recognized as one-time "clients" of the court but who registered no reciprocal recall of an earlier acquaintance with him. The initial bond may not have been that strong, or it had been one-sided, or they were not individuals for whom "people connections" held much interest. They simply did not remember him; he had, after all, changed with the years too.

Finally, there were those few whose expressions might flicker brief, ruminating recognition, but within whom some bitterness must still reside, whose memories must be unhappy ones or with whom personal conflicts had gone unresolved, for they would quickly look away and pass on by.

Toward none in the latter two groups did Kelly initiate a greeting, even though he might feel eager to know something of their present lives. His relationship with them had been official and confidential rather than social, and that did not accord him the privilege of taking even a simple step of greeting that might be regarded as intrusion. Some sleeping dogs are to be let lie.

Smither's Drug Store was one of Kelly's hometown landmarks that was still unchanged but very much alive. Since the time of even Kelly's adolescence it had been a vital social hub of the community, far more significant than just a place to buy razor blades or get a prescription filled.

Running partway along one side of the narrow store was a soda fountain of fine, '30s-era, "streamline" design, a combination of shaped wood, shiny chrome, and mirrors whose design and quality of finish exceeded that of any other commercial fixtures in town. At its counter, eighteen patrons, most of them known to each other, could sit on elevated, leather-upholstered swivel chairs. Extending back from the fountain to the rear of the long room under a high ceiling of geometrically patterned pressed tin was a double row of booths, brightly canopied with red and white canvas to resemble a patio cafe.

It was a pleasant place; the help and the patrons were congenial. As it had been for years, it was still The Place for people from along

Main Street to drop in for a Coke or to have the luncheon special. What one got there was more than the food or refreshments bought and paid for: one left with a feeling of amounting to something with people who mattered, a renewed validation of one's own worthy membership in the mainstream of the town. For a few moments, at least, you felt you were somebody. With perhaps an even greater need for self-confirmation, high school kids took over the booths in late afternoons and evenings and, between laughter and adolescent ostentation, gobbled ice cream sodas, gooey sundaes, and other rich concoctions.

Sid Smithers, the vigilant, bustling store owner, knew virtually everyone in town and buoyantly hailed patrons by their full names as they came and went. He seldom missed a one. His greeting was a special moment of the day, like having one's personal pennant run up the flagpole.

And so every summer Kelly renewed his patronage of the store for old time's sake, for the continuing vitality of the place, and for the satisfaction that he felt in Mr. Smither's jaunty welcome from behind the prescription desk: "Hello, Jim Kelly! About time you're getting back here!" It was as if he'd never been away.

"Good to see you, Sid. Still peddling pills, are you? Your store looks better than ever."

At noon on one such day, after the pleasantries with Sid, Kelly eased over to the one vacant stool at the fountain. At his left, a man in a red plaid shirt of western cut with pearl-like snaps instead of buttons agreeably hunched a little extra room for him to step up and settle in, saying through a mouthful of food, "Always room for one more." And the two of them continued the light conversation of congenials in close proximity.

"Thanks for makin' room. Great day, isn't it!"

"Yeah. Good weather for the county fair comin' up."

"Oh, that's right. It's fair time again, isn't it?"

"Sure is. They're gonna have a good one this year!"

On the run, a smiling, wholesome-looking blonde waitress in a crisp yellow uniform dress with dark brown sailor's collar handed Kelly a menu and set a glass of icewater at his place without needing to be asked. "Here ya go!" she sparkled in brief but direct contact, during which Kelly's comfort and satisfaction seemed to be her sole concern. "The luncheon blue plate special's clipped on the front of the menu there, and the regular items are inside," she said. "I'll be right back to take your order."

Making little jabs of his fork at the food on his plate, the man in the plaid shirt said, "If you're hungry they got a real good do on the meatloaf special today."

"Hmmm . . . does look good," said Kelly, scanning the menu without much comprehension. His mind was compulsively searching elsewhere. He was sure he'd known the boy who had become this stocky, balding man beside him; something jovially audacious in the expression of his eyes and some slight mannerism of his speech–just a hint of a lisp–were distinctive traits that rang a bell. In the man's good nature, too, there was a shade of familiarity indicating, it seemed, a guarded recognition of Kelly, but since the man made no overt acknowledgment of acquaintance, Kelly stuck to small talk, offering no self-introduction; he felt constrained from saying, "Shouldn't I know you from someplace?" although he was quite sure of it.

The waitress bounced back, raising her eyebrows and tilting her head, inviting Kelly's order.

"I'll have to go with the meatloaf on recommendation of my partner here," said Kelly.

"Good choice. Freddy'd never steer you wrong. He knows what's good, doncha Freddy?"

Freddy. The name was a clue that Kelly pondered. "His name is Freddy . . . but Freddy who? What should I know about him?"

Conversation between the two men slacked off as Kelly dug into his blue plate special and Freddy finished off a sherbet dish of strawberry jello and whipped cream.

"Well, eat hearty," said Freddy, wiping his chin with a paper napkin. "I gotta get rollin'. Got a truckload of repairs to get out to my mill in Ashley Draw, and I'd better get her there pronto or my crew'll raise the devil with me. They want to finish up the overhaul so they can take Friday off for the fair. Nice seein' you," he said, just short, it seemed, of adding "again" and stepped down from the counter.

Over the luncheon noises, Kelly heard Mr. Smithers call out, "See you, Freddy Swanson!" to the departing mill owner in a tone that took for granted the man's imminent return to the store. "Take it easy in the woods this afternoon!"

"Swanson. Did Sid say Swanson?" thought Kelly. "Of course . . . that is Fred Swanson–he *is* somebody I have known. But how he has changed! It all comes back to me. What a scrawny-kid handful he was when I had him; nothing stocky or bald-headed about him then!"

As an adolescent on probation, Fred had been under Kelly's wing for a year or more; first for the theft of beer from a beer truck and then for vandalism. These were the kinds of details that Kelly never forgot.

When the boy had first been referred to the juvenile court by the county sheriff, Kelly was struck by the kid's foreboding start: born on December 7, 1941, at about the same time, as far as anyone could tell, that his father was manning a forty millimeter antiaircraft battery aboard the USS Oklahoma at Pearl Harbor. The young sailor had never made it home to his wife and son. By the time Freddy was in high school and Kelly got into the act there was a stepfather, an enterprising but ornery cuss of a woodsman whose guts the kid always claimed to hate.

Fred then was a bright, rambunctious, happy-go-lucky nut, not a psychopath and not really of a criminal nature, but a Huck Finn sort whose one great interest was cars. Well, cars and girls. But most girls didn't like him because all he could talk about was cars.

The beer offense had not been the end of the world, not too serious a thing, but the vandalism was pretty bad. Fred and another kid had knocked out more than 200 eight-by-ten-inch panes of glass from the cottage-style windows of a planing mill that stood at the western edge of town on a spur of the Great Northern Railroad. While engrossed in throwing stones they were reported by a passer-by, and the sheriff–a sour sort who took all kids' offenses as a personal affront–soon hauled them in, as they certainly deserved to be. The mill owners, big frogs in this small community puddle, were understandably irate and demanded a commitment of the pair to the state reform school.

At the hearing where the boys, in the presence of their parents and the county attorney, readily admitted their guilt, the down-to-earth, bespectacled, aging judge sat silent for a few moments in his cluttered chambers. Taking up his curved pipe, knocking it free of ashes, he tamped in a fresh wad of Prince Albert with a sooty forefinger and lit up, sweet-smelling smoke swirling about his head. When he had his pipe going was when he seemed to get his important thinking done.

"You know," he said in a conversational tone, "this was a pretty dang fool thing you boys did. There's a lot of people upset about it and I can't blame them. If somebody knocked out my windows I'd be pretty sore too. Now they want me to send you away to the state reform school. That may be just what I should do. . . . "

Turning in his swivel chair, he seemed to absent himself from the room and sat puffing, looking out across the courthouse park for some long moments while the guilty pair awaited his decision in sickly suspense. Turning to rejoin the small assemblage, mechanically replacing his pipe on the abalone shell ashtray before him, he spoke as though there had been no interruption: "There's two things wrong with that. One is that I haven't seen reform school do many boys much good. And the other is . . . " he pursed his lips contemplatively for another long moment, " . . . the other is . . . that if I send you away that leaves all of those broken windows unfixed. . . . " Looking directly into the eyes of one boy and then the other, he said, "I don't think that you should get away with leaving a costly mess like that." Shifting his attention to the parents, he continued, "So I'm not going to send them away. Not now anyway.

"You all know my probation officer here, Mr. Kelly. I'm going to turn you boys over to him, and I want him to see what he can do with you. The first thing that you've got to do is make it right with the people at the mill for all of that broken glass. And I want Mr. Kelly to keep me informed of what you do about that. So that'll be all for today. You can go home with your folks now. I'll just take your case under advisement."

That had all happened before the days when restitution had been "discovered," touted, and bureaucratized. What Kelly did was simply and quite boldly propose to Fred's disbelieving stepfather that the man loan the boys enough money to buy replacement glass and putty so they could get started on the repair of the vandalized windows at once. "You've got the money," Kelly told the man. "I can't personally guarantee that you'll get it back, but I intend that the boys shall repay you, and nobody else should have to foot the bill." The old man's response was pretty gruff, but he came through with a loan of something over $300. Then, with the boys in tow, Kelly rounded up chisels, putty knives and other tools, and ladders. The three of them spent the better part of four days high up along the mill's outer walls cleaning the old rock-hard putty from the sashes, then pointing in and glazing new panes of glass.

It took the boys a while to catch on to the use of a putty knife, but they had good hands, Kelly was patient, and they soon took a measure of pride in their work–egged on by an element of competition not too subtly introduced by their overseer: "Let's see which one of you can catch on the fastest and do the best job here. And no sloppy stuff; we'll be here until this job is done right."

After they got the glass properly replaced, it took two more days to painstakingly brush two coats of white paint onto all of the sashes and narrow mullions, a more tedious and exacting job even than puttying.

By that time the twosome and their probation officer had gotten pretty well acquainted. There was a comfortable rapport among them much as that between a competent coach and the youthful members of a good sports team. In short, they liked one another, the boys respecting Kelly–he absolutely meant what he said, but he had a sense of humor and you could talk to him–and for his part, Kelly saw in the boys' intelligence and energy the solid potential to amount to something once they got beyond the bumpy crossties of adolescence.

The mill owners, skeptical at first, were so surprised and pleased with the outcome of the work project that they backed off on their criticism of the judge for not shipping the bloomin' kids right off to reform school. On his own, the mill manager ("I did some dumb things as a kid myself, but I never got caught. . . . ") offered the boys enough Saturday work in the company woodlot to pay off Fred's old man for the loan.

It took several months of weekend work to pay off the debt, but when accomplished, the troublemakers exuberantly proclaimed that their period of probation should be considered over.

"Guess we won't need to be checkin' in with you no more, Mr. Kelly! We got 'er all wrapped up now—cleaned up our mess, paid off our debt, and we're free! Right?"

"Hey, hey, hey . . . " Kelly extravagantly responded. "You guys must have got brain damage from overexposure to the sun while you were up there working on those windows. You did that job well, real well, but you've still got some unfinished business to take care of. Graduation is only two-and-a-half months away, and the school people tell me that it's an open question whether or not either one of you will make the grade. Now, we'll get around to talking about signing off probation when I see each one of you with a diploma in your hands. For the next ten weeks you get in here to my office to study three times a week. If I'm not here my secretary will be. She'll be expecting you, and I'll be checking with her. And don't give her a bad time. We'll make something respectable out of you guys yet."

There were groans and expressions of righteous disbelief. "Aw jeez, Mr. Kelly . . . " But that's the way it was.

And things worked out all right. The boys studied, got their grades up to passing or better, earned their diplomas, and soon after graduation each one went his separate way, on to new interests, new adventures and responsibilities. For Fred that had meant enlistment in the Navy, partly out of a sentimental desire to follow in the footsteps of his real dad.

That had been," thought Kelly . . . "could it really be? . . . twenty-three years ago . . . "

He swallowed the last of his coffee, which by now was cold, and relinquished his seat to another customer. Preparing to pay his bill, he walked to the counter of cigarettes and candy at the front of the store where Mrs. Smithers, though grown a bit arthritic, still worked as the noontime cashier.

"You don't owe anything, Jim," Mrs. Smithers smiled. "Freddy paid for your lunch. And he said to tell you to come on out and help repair some windows at his mill this afternoon. Said you're an expert and would know what he meant. I guess that's an inside story, huh?"

"Well, I'll be!" said Kelly. "Thanks for the message. Yeah, that's an inside story; and I'm no longer in the window repair business!"

So it was confirmed: he'd got the story right. Fred Swanson's who his lunch partner was all right, and there was still a streak of the devilish kid in him! Kelly'd hit the jackpot in his personal-reacquaintance lottery once again. Which was about as much of a bonus as his kind of work ever paid. And thanks, he'd settle for that.

The Hearing

My job in the women's prison was an administrative experiment. I was the first male to be assigned to the executive staff, where I took charge of all of the treatment services plus those dealing with the intake of new inmates.

There were, to be sure, other men on the staff. The front gate was manned around the clock by two male officers. The boiler room had twenty-four-hour oversight by male stationary engineers. And there was a plumber and a carpenter. The officers and the engineers had no direct association with inmates, but the plumber and the carpenter each had female inmate helpers, and you can bet that they were watched by female staff members against hanky-panky in any of the countless out-of-the-way places to which their work often took them.

My assignment had not resulted from routine procedures of the departmental personnel office, but had been initiated by the director of the Department of Corrections, the top man, with very careful scrutiny of my credentials and character. To be honest, I enjoyed all of the attention. I was happily married, and I had full confidence in my own motives in agreeing to work in a setting of females—many of whom were totally without scruples—and took it all as an adventure and a chance to prove my stuff.

Before assuming my new duties, I had not anticipated quite as much of a stir as my presence created. Although my principal responsibilities had more to do with staff than directly with the inmates, I was soon besieged with the latter's chits—written notes—requesting appointments with me. Some of the more brazen or desperate women, eschewing the required formality of written requests, would nab me, seductively, beseechingly, or even threateningly as I moved about the prison on the errands of my work. Their requests arose in part, I think, from curiosity about the new male addition, but more seriously, others arose from the hope that a fresh personality might be a better listener than incumbent counselors or that, because of my position, I might have more power to respond to requests or complaints of injustice. Or as a new guy I might be more susceptible to manipulation on behalf of someone's questionable or outright improper agenda. I was determined that truly legitimate needs should not go unattended, but sorting them out from the con jobs was sometimes a chore.

Generally, I felt that I was off to a good start, learning new routines and the features of a women's prison, which were quite different from those of a prison for men. I had some very competent staff members, and I enjoyed making new friends.

A professional relationship that proved rewarding over the months began unexpectedly on my very first day; it was unusual in that it was with a person outside of my own department. Her name was Helen Grady–Mrs. Helen Grady–and she was a correctional officer, a guard under older terminology.

Traditionally, correctional officers are apt to be suspicious and mistrustful of treatment personnel and vice versa for reasons, or perhaps emotions, that we don't need to get into here. Suffice to say that, while employees in the administratively separate treatment and custodial divisions both work for the same employer, they are apt to dance to quite different philosophical drummers. Grady–no one called her Mrs. or Helen, it was always Grady–was not like that. She had a way of looking past uniforms and titles to the person within the cloak, a refreshing and admirable quality.

It was the warden who introduced me to Grady. In the course of my orientation, Warden Mary Williams, a wonderfully energetic, bright, good-humored, middle-aged lady, walked me to the office that was to be mine. Just as we reached the door there appeared from the patients' waiting room across the hall a figure looking a lot like a very large English bulldog walking on its hind legs.

"Oh, here's Grady," said Warden Williams with a friendly this-is-a-happy-event smile. "Grady, I want you to meet Mr. Rosen. He's finally got here and you will no doubt be seeing a lot of him."

I liked Grady's twinkling Irish sauciness immediately as she said, "So now I've got to keep track of a good-looking man in this place surrounded by all of these females!"

"Thanks. I guess that's a compliment, but maybe it's me you'll have to protect!" I said, and we were off on the start of a warm, mutually respectful, often bantering relationship. Grady and I joshed on the same wavelength.

During those initial days in Grady's custodial domain, I often found her at my open office door, shaking her homely head and, with a wry smile, pretending disbelief and forbearance. She greatly enjoyed the fact that I had been forbidden–by the director no less–to close my office door until a long opening had been cut in the solid white birch slab and glazed with clear, wire-reinforced glass. "Wise move," said Grady. "The director knows the score. With the door open I can look in and watch out for my girls!" The implication was that "her girls" were irreproachable patsies and that I was a potential evil-doer.

Her spoofing caution and exaggerated disapproval were a welcome contrast to the too-forced cordiality and the I-really-feel-more-like-throwing-up smiles of the female department heads, most of whom could barely contain their angry, paranoid resentment of my presence with them on the executive staff. Incidentally, I never heard Grady gossip about any of those women or badmouth any of her superiors, but it became clear that she did not share their resentment of me; she was entirely comfortable with me while most of them were not. During one unusual, rather irregular situation in which I was later quite dramatically involved with an inmate, Grady was literally at my side with remarkable sensitivity and wisdom.

Grady's principal duty, with the assistance of one junior officer, was to patrol the long, gleamingly waxed hallway that formed the core of the single-story administration building, the clinical services wing, and the reception center, connecting them in a long arc. Doorways along the extended thoroughfare opened to the warden's office; a large conference room in which groups, including the parole board, met; the records and business offices; an employee's dining room; doctors', dentists', psychologists', and counselors' offices; and a multifaith chapel. It was Grady's job to see that no unauthorized inmates got into or out of this extended area, that they behaved while they were legitimately there, and that noise was held to a reasonable level, especially in the waiting room, which was a large, pleasant alcove off the main hall. Altogether, it was a job requiring patience and firmness; inmates with personal problems awaiting a doctor or dentist, a counselor or a chaplain, can be emotional, sometimes even hysterical. It is essential that they be controlled by means that maintain a low decibel level and do not provoke physical, more disturbing responses.

In twenty years as a correctional officer Grady had seen the worst of the human creature, but to her credit, she had never gone sour, never burned out as some long-term prison employees have been known to do. Through some special gift she had a remarkable ability to direct and supervise female inmates. To start with, her physical appearance was an asset, signaling restraint and moderation to anyone around her. Her height was only average, but she was solid, with wide shoulders, a watermelon bosom, massive arms and buttocks. Her head was large, flat-faced, with chin and full neck all in one, like a large, inverted pickle jar. Slightly protruding, hooded eyes were always watery. As she strolled her beat, hands clasped behind her back, her bulky bearing presented an unmistakable expectation of order. I never heard her raise her voice in anger, never saw her lift a hand, but she calmly conducted business with the absolute certainty that whatever she asked or directed would be done. In Grady this was neither threat nor arrogance. It was the woman's special gift: supreme confidence, not so much in herself–she seemed rather selfless–but that her expectations would be honored. The contrast of her Mack-truck body with her low-key reasonability was unique, like a female pope in a football linebacker's outfit.

Even more special was Grady's great interest in people–almost all people around her–and the impressive intuition that she had about them. Stoically, she knew the certain need for firm control of predatory personalities, and she exercised it; this was in recognition of a prison reality that was untainted by anger or hatred, somewhat like a successful circus trainer who knows the dangerous potential of the animals that he tends and loves. On the other hand, for the weak and inadequate–the "motherless"–she was understanding and appropriately supportive, subtly offering welcome reassurance with a simple nod of her head, a light touch on the arm, or a quiet word of praise.

One of Grady's significant collateral duties was the supervision of three inmates whose work assignment, as succinctly noted in their records, was "cleaning detail–Grady." In addition to keeping the long hallway spotless, each of these "girls" had charge of cleaning a certain number of the offices along it. It may be surprising, but it was generally not difficult to find women who were fully trustworthy to work quite independently in and out of offices in this way. They were, of course, never allowed to work without close oversight in such sensitive areas as the records office, where inmate records were kept, or in medical offices, where there might be access to drugs.

Without engendering improper, overly personalized relationships, Grady supervised her three girls with a kind of sustaining buoyancy. At breaks in their work she would often sit with one or more of them, relax, smoke, have a cup of coffee or tea and chat. This not only resulted in good work performance, but Grady's genuine, though unobtrusive, warmth and perceptiveness were highly regarded. Some of her charges needed and drew more from her–her good listening, tempered outlook, sensible support–than others. One of these whom I came to know and be fond of was Helen Davis, her first name coincidentally the same as Grady's.

Without showing favoritism, Grady took an especially strong interest in Helen. Over the weeks one saw that, in Grady, Helen had found a responsive friend from whom she received what might technically be called "supportive counseling" in a most natural way, a way that few trained counselors could provide in their often self-conscious, artificial environments. Sometimes, in human relationships, the heart may be wiser than the head.

By chance, it was Helen who was my office cleaner. And I soon came to appreciate the quality of her work as well as her pleasant nature. How many inmates would have liked to have her job; in close proximity with their top-most keepers, hopeful that a few crumbs of special attention or favor might fall from the official hands that controlled their lives! Unlike them, Helen was never presumptuous or intrusive.

She would knock on my door, pop her head in, and, with a smile as bright as a meadowlark on a woven wire fence, ask, "Okay if I come in now?"

If I agreed, she would bustle in with, "Isn't this a nice day?" or, "You look snowed under–I'll only be a minute," or, "How could your windows have gotten so dirty? Must have been that rain storm. If you can let me know when you're going to be out for a while I'll get them washed up good without disturbing you."

She was jackstraw-thin with wrinkly skin and bony elbows. Her frizzy brown hair, streaked with gray, unbecomingly cut in a style once called "bobbed," gave her a quality of a rather frightened, obsequious little girl, though she must have been in her mid-forties. Her sunken, pale cheeks were deeply lined, but bright blue eyes flashed intelligence and humor, making her smile appealing–not with the come-on of a "Hey, baby! I've-got-pleasures-for-you" solicitress, but of a vulnerable child. She would quickly dust and tidy up the place, be gone for a moment, then return with flowers freshly cut from the prison gardens and artfully arranged for a spot on the corner of my desk.

I was jealous of my office time; the flow of paper was often overwhelming, and I needed time to myself to deal with it. For this reason, while I surely did not intend rudeness, I seldom got into much small talk with Helen. Occasionally, perhaps on a Monday morning, I might say, "Well, how was the country club over the weekend?"

And she'd reply, "Oh, it was really swingin'. You can't believe the wild parties!" Which, of course, was a denial of how dull the place was, and we'd laugh and both be on about our business. I don't recall that she ever asked me anything of a personal nature; beyond simple cordiality, she never made any attempt to get to me on her own behalf.

Over the weeks and months, however, I was not oblivious to a more troubled quality in this spirited personality. When she was at her work, independent of my presence, I noticed that her sunshine faded quickly to a heavy, almost grim, seriousness. She tore into her chores compulsively in a way that I first assumed was a ready escape from the life around her; but I came to see that it was more than that, almost like a beaded curtain subconsciously contrived to hold within, while screening out from others, the knowledge of some great personal despair whose weight obsessed her. I did indeed wonder at that secret burden from time to time, but it would have been quite improper for me to inquire. Then one day, as a result of a chance conversation with Grady, I learned the details of the mystery.

Once in a while, without planning, Grady and I would brown-bag lunch together, she sitting in an armchair on one side of my desk, me on the other, each of us facing the well-tended rose garden in the very pleasant courtyard just outside of the steel-framed casement windows. It was a welcome change from the dining room, which was fine–good meals, cheap prices–but eating in there daily with one's departmental workmates got incestuous; one needed some variety. Grady usually had a new story or two, never far off-color–she didn't like those–and she really enjoyed telling them. She had a wonderfully hearty laugh, too, which was very infectious and made a good story even better. We'd talk, not about heavy stuff, but about her dog, who was her sole housemate (I never knew what had become of her husband), surf fishing, which she loved, my sailboat, and gardening.

In this way one noon we somehow got to talking about Grady's cleaning girls and her responsibility for supervising them. I commented that she had an unusual relationship with them, especially with Helen, where there seemed to be a lot of mutual respect.

"Yes. I've never had an inmate quite like Helen," she said. "She never gives me any problem–she doesn't raise any problem in your office, does she?" and without waiting for an answer, asked, "Do you know her story?"

"No. I've never even looked at her file. She's always very proper in my office, a self-effacing little mouse really. Yet, you know, I sense something quite pathetic about her."

"Yeah," said Grady. "Pathetic. That's a good word." It was not like us to get into this sort of thing, but, uncharacteristically, Grady told me the story.

"Helen's different," Grady said. "Unlike most inmates I've known because she's not bitter about having been sent to prison. Oh, I don't mean that she likes it here; sometimes she's despondent about her loss of freedom. But you know, she's the first person to say that the local authorities had been pretty patient with her before they shipped her off."

"Pretty rare," I agreed. "How come?"

"Well," Grady said, "Helen was convicted of a string of paper-hanging charges. She wrote a lot of bad checks over several years, and that is society's problem with her. But the root of it all is her problem with herself, which is alcoholism. Helen's not a crook: she's a lush. She never wanted to harm anyone or steal from them. What she wanted was a drink, and then another and another, and of course she has no tolerance for booze. She'll tell you right out that she can't drink. But even so–merciful God, does she know!–that even now there's nothing she'd like more than a drink. And she'll tell you, too–she's got a good sense of humor–that she'd write a check to get one!"

From Helen's appearance I'd already guessed that she was an alcoholic. But you don't get sent to prison for being a drunk. It's what you do while under the influence that puts you away. I'd never stopped to wonder what crimes had landed Helen in here. "So," I said to Grady, "Helen has the double whammy: one, an addiction to alcohol, and the other, an addiction to checks. She's broke and needs a drink so she writes a check to pay for it; but one drink isn't enough, just leads to more. Then, when she sobers up, she feels guilty about the check, downs a few hairs of the dog to drown the worry, and starts all over again."

"That's the story," Grady agreed. "You've seen the pattern a thousand times I know. But here's the sad part. Helen raises some breed of small, exotic dogs that sell for a lot of money. Those dogs were her life; she loved them like they were her kids. Being away from them now and worrying about them is her worst punishment. It's also a financial disaster because without good care they won't be there to make Helen's living when she's done her time. She's not one who's going to turn a trick or steal or push drugs for a living.

"While Helen was awaiting trial before getting sent here, she was held for three months at the county jail–you know how the courts are backed up. During that time, Helen's mother, with whom she lived, looked after the dogs as best she could, though she was too infirm to groom them properly or see to selling them. Then, two weeks after Helen was checked in here, the old lady had a stroke and died. So then Helen's brother, also an alcoholic, moved into the mother's house with promises to tend the dogs, but he was totally undependable. Some of the dogs he practically gave away to raise wine money; the others he neglected so that the humane society had to take them. You think you got troubles!"

This combination of events and circumstances then, explained the pathos that I'd sensed behind the curtain of Helen's daily, congenial routine. "But you hear so many tales in prison, Grady. Sad tales designed to get sympathy and special consideration."

"Hey, don't I know that!" Grady reacted. "But this is no con job. Only bit by bit did Helen tell me her story. She was hurting, and we talked about it. Just to be sure, I drove over to Hampton on the QT on my day off and checked it out—unofficially of course. It's true. It's all true."

"You're something else, Grady! A real bleeding heart in an officer's uniform!" I said, faking sarcasm. But inside I was thinking, "What a jewel this funny-looking lady is."

Helen's sustaining hope was that she would be given an early parole. And she was surprisingly realistic about her future. What she'd told Grady was, "I don't blame them for not trusting me. I can't trust myself. What I would like to do is get a job somewhere like in an animal shelter, have a good parole agent I could talk to like I can talk to you and who'd keep close track of me; and then if they'd help me stay on a chemical antialcohol deal like Antabuse, I can make it. I want to make it. I've got to make it!"

In this state, a convicted offender is sentenced to prison by a court, but the state parole board has considerable discretion in determining just how long a period of time an inmate shall serve within the walls. Customarily, an offender will be seen initially by the board within a few weeks of her arrival at the prison. Almost never will a parole date be set at that first meeting, but another hearing date will be set for a year hence; at that second hearing a relatively minor offender is quite likely to be scheduled for release on parole on a date soon thereafter. Presently Helen was holding herself together by concentrating on the outcome of her second hearing, now just four weeks away. If she could get out soon, she might be able to yet salvage something from her mother's modest estate and somehow regain at least a pair of her dogs and make a new start.

I found the story and Grady's carefully balanced interest in it quite impressive—touching, really. Grady was not one to go overboard, but it was obvious that she had come to believe that if ever an inmate deserved early parole it was Helen. She was wise enough not to encourage false hope by telling Helen that, however. We agreed, too, that we were both powerless bystanders; there was nothing we could legitimately do to influence a parole board decision. Theirs was a jealously guarded prerogative for which they were solely responsible, sometimes painfully so, to the public; even our own warden, a woman of great strength with a realistic knowledge about inmates, would never offer the board a recommendation except in the very rare instance of a member's request.

After hearing the story, my exchanges with Helen in the following days were automatically, if subtly, altered. As I've said, it would have been improper of me to talk with her about her case. But I made a little more of a point to express my appreciation to her for her care of my office needs. I showed a little more joy at the flowers that she brought each day; I inquired which were her heaviest workdays, which offices were most difficult to care for. The topics were impersonal, but human contact was extended.

Helen responded warmly in kind; without ever stepping over the invisible line of discretion, she got in bits of her own brand of Irish humor: "You're going to need new carpet in here pretty soon, Mr. Rosen. This is getting mighty worn; my vacuum cleaner is getting plugged up from it. But maybe you'll get paroled first," she joked, "and you won't have to worry about it." Or, more seriously, "I heard that eight new girls came in today, Mr. Rosen. Where are you going to stack them?"

Nevertheless, four weeks moved along quickly—for me—and I rather forgot that Helen's moment before the board was about here. The week of the board meeting was a wild one. Two of our counselors, whom we really needed, were out sick; there were still records to be readied for the board. Receiving had filled alarmingly to dangerous doubling-up; disciplinary infractions were on the rise. An inmate being held on a death sentence for a particularly heinous murder was moved to one of the men's prisons for execution, and that had the inmates very upset—the state was actually going to "off" a woman? The times were busy, requiring some twelve-hour days. My contacts with Helen during the period were courteous, certainly, but fleeting. There was simply no time for small talk.

On Wednesday afternoon, Helen, most unlike her, entered my office without knocking. In a freckled hand she was carrying a bowl of unusually bright, firm, yellow rosebuds, which she placed rather ceremoniously on my desk, looking at me with a shy expectancy. For an instant I felt irritated. I did not want to be bothered now, had no energy for admiring these gorgeous miracles of nature and no time to engage in uncharacteristic pleasantries, which Helen seemed to be inviting.

Like a camera shutter, the deep blue, little-girl eyes in the wrinkled face flickered hurt; Helen had sensed my impatience and was quick to explain. "Excuse me for bursting in, Mr. Rosen. I won't be in tomorrow. I go for my hearing with the board. So I wanted to get your flowers changed today. These will have to do you until Friday."

Oh, God. I hated myself in that moment. I had forgotten that tomorrow was her hearing day. Her whole life was on the line. Why shouldn't she have presumed a contact with me, a free person of generally good will, for a supportive word, maybe even some magical reassurance? In a board hearing lasting only a few minutes, the status of her freedom, the shape of her life, was going to be determined by utter strangers.

"Oh, Helen!" I said, throwing down my pencil and leaning back in my chair. "Forgive me! Of course you go to the board tomorrow. How long it has taken for this day to come."

I was tempted to say more, to encourage her, to say, "I'm sure it will be okay. You're certain to get a date. You'll be going home soon!" But of course I could not. Such assurances would be stupid. How could I know what the outcome would be?

"Keep your fingers crossed for me?" she asked.

"Helen, you can count on it. Every time I look at those roses, I'll say a magic word. I don't know how strong my magic is, but I sincerely wish you well before the board." I meant it.

Like Grady, I did strongly hope that the board would recognize that Helen was no menacing criminal but a woman seriously afflicted. Keeping her on ice in prison did protect the public from her drunken episodes and the related inexcusable checks. But no one could say that there was much going on in here that was going to help her with her alcoholism. She would do better under a strict regimen outside. And there was the matter of her love for her dogs and the fact that this one great positive in her life was being destroyed. Even the most unforgiving of prosecuting attorneys, totally sour on human nature, might give a damn about the animals!

When I arrived at work the next morning, the long main corridor was busier than usual. The atmosphere was charged with some voiceless expectation, as though a parade were soon to begin. The ladies in the records office were dressed in their best. A table apart from the others in the dining room was already being set with a linen cloth and polished silver for the board members' luncheon. The knowledge that it was "board day" pervaded the institution; there was an aura of impending Judgement. Even inmates who were not scheduled for the board dreamt of somehow being favorably noticed by a board member and winning a storybook approval. Younger staff members, too, charged with detailed preparations for the board's work, were hopeful of favorable comments supporting aspirations for career advancement.

As I walked down the hall I caught a glimpse of Grady "on patrol" among a group of twenty or so inmates at sick call in the doctors' waiting room, but we had no chance to exchange a greeting. At my desk the bouquet of yellow rosebuds, now opening in their fluted, black glass vase, cued me to think of Helen and wish her well. Then I immersed myself in a huge pile of paperwork and bore down. The morning passed without noteworthy incident and hardly an interruption. Before I knew it the noon hour had arrived.

Feeling good about all of the work I had finished, I headed for the dining room, astonished for a moment at how quiet the corridor had become. Even on board day all inmates had to return to their cottages for the noon count and lunch, leaving the passageway and the waiting room deserted. It was a welcome calm.

Approaching the dining room in the administration building, I could hear a murmur of voices and smell the appetizing aroma of barbecue sauce. There was always a special menu for board day and I was suddenly very hungry. It would be nice to have a really good lunch.

At the dining room entrance I heard, from some distance further along the hall, the metallic thunk of the exit bar on the heavy boardroom door and saw the door push open, just opposite the warden's office. From behind it there hunched a spare figure in a plain, prison-issue, pink cotton dress, a black cardigan sweater, and cheap, black, loafer-type slippers. I felt my jaw drop as I recognized Helen and saw her lurch alarmingly against the green, epoxied block wall, convulsing and near collapse, struggling to stretch the lower portion of her sweater up over her head. The outcome of the hearing was sickeningly obvious.

"Helen!" I called, running to catch hold of her. From within the woolen shroud she recognized me briefly with wet blue eyes, then covered up, keening primitively. I extended an arm around her tiny waist, and taking a grip on one bony elbow with my other hand, I led her back along the hallway to the records office across from, but out of sight of, the dining room. "They denied me. . . . They denied me," she cried softly.

Relieved to find the office unoccupied, I embraced Helen tightly with both arms, pulling her close to me as she went limp with wrenching sobs. At that moment she could have been my own child: that's how I responded, like a father, although I'm younger than she. My guts were torn by her distress, and I was angry, disbelieving of the news.

Just how long I'd held her, being otherwise quite helpless, when there came the sound of footsteps from the hallway, I'm not sure. Probably less than two minutes, but it seemed much longer. I braced myself for the arrival of what I feared could be a startled, and quite likely scandalized, observer. Should it be Mrs. Wiedenbacher, the obese, truculent records officer who always looked to me like a gathering thunderstorm, the sight of me holding an inmate in my arms could well trigger a horrified response audible clear out to the front gate. The very best I could hope from her, I thought, was a low rumble and a change of course directly to the warden's office, there to shrilly proclaim that her predictions of the evils certain to befall the prison on the inclusion of a male (with all of his inevitably base proclivities) on the staff was being disgustingly enacted at this very minute . . . in her very own office! For an irrational instant a streak of rebel in me welcomed the confrontation. It was time for a showdown with Wiedenbacher.

One of the problems, just one of the problems, of a prison is that, continually surrounded and beset by serious, even gross, characterological distortions, without enough hours in the day, without enough manpower, without enough certain knowledge, and with emotional energy that has its limits, staff members sometimes become desensitized and give up: they retreat to a moated affect whose drawbridges to humanity are seldom lowered. Thus, the captors become captives too, sour and broken, doing time, doing time. Maybe too self-righteously (but, damn it, I'm human too) I'd long ago put the records officer in this category.

But it was not the records officer who appeared, and fortunately, her outraged reaction did not occur. The face that showed in the doorway was not Wiedenbacher's but that of my bulldog friend, correctional officer Helen M. Grady, on routine reconnaissance of her extensive territory.

A look of questioning surprise lighted her rheumy eyes for an instant, then quickly moderated, and she gave a nod of full comprehension. Without unclasping her massive arms from behind her back, she nodded once again, briefly closing her eyelids in a signal of disappointment and disbelief at her perceived outcome of the hearing and of her warm approval of my embrace of an inmate–an acquaintance, a human being, yes, a kind of friend–in pain. There was no need for words between us; intuitively, Grady knew what was necessary: time and seclusion, which she took it on herself to guarantee. Ponderously, she turned her bulk and edged left to take a stand just outside of the doorway, where all I could see of her was the fleshy elbow of her right arm.

This was an anomalous moment in which the taken-for-granted roles of three people in a prison were markedly altered. Here, instead of coarse and predacious, was an inmate completely distraught, helpless, in response to a devastating disappointment. Here was a correctional officer whose customary duty was unrelenting surveillance and control, but who now stood as a kindly, imperturbable sentinel, sheltering a human breakdown. And here too was a male prison administrator holding a woman inmate in a compassionate embrace. But tell me, if a prison is to do more than punish, that is, if a prison, in addition to isolating, controlling, and punishing, is also to reform, rebuild, and regenerate, how is it to do so in ignorance and rejection of the gentler emotions?

Whether there was any further traffic in the hallway or whether Grady barred anyone from entering the records office in the next few moments I don't know; I never thought to ask her later and she did not say. What I do know is, simply, that she was there, sensitively attuned and appropriately prepared to shield the sight of a very personal situation, one decently elemental but terribly foreign to this place, from the view of the misunderstanding, the willfully distorting, the bigoted, or the curious until the helpless woman in my arms–Helen, a convicted felon, one of our mutual charges–had recovered sufficiently to allow the two of us to get her to the clinic and a kindly, aging doctor who had never lost the capacity to care.

An Uncommon Task

After a seventy-mile drive along the winding coastal road, the warden pulled into the basement garage of his modest beach-house. With the top down the air had been refreshingly clear and pleasantly warm, but now it was good to be at his destination. "Beach-house" really was a misnomer, for the house was not on the beach. It stood on a green, far-sweeping bluff some three or four hundred feet above the Pacific shoreline.

Stepping slowly from the car, he took a basket of fresh fruit from the rear seat and carried it a short distance across the driveway, turning to follow a pathway leading to the rustic, tree-hidden caretaker's cottage where an aging but alert Filipino couple met him on the porch with joyful dignity. He had not phoned ahead, but they were expecting him.

"Hello, warden. Welcome, welcome! We listen to da news reports on noon radio and we sure you be coming!"

"Hello, my friends! Yes, yes, here I am. Here, I brought you some fresh fruit from the Santa Rosa Market," he said, handing up the basket of bright oranges, bananas, and grapes.

Following the affectionate exchange, the warden turned back toward the main house. This is the way it was at those times when he came here by himself.

Climbing the circular wooden staircase from the garage to the living room, the warden was once again struck by the magnificence of the view framed in the front wall of glass. Beyond the richly foliaged overlook swept a humbling expanse of blue ocean whose horizon arced from due south on the left to just west of north on the right. The large, comfortably furnished room itself was welcoming. The caretakers had been there earlier and left the sliding doors to the deck ajar, allowing passage of the freshening sea breeze; and on the coffee table and the fireplace mantle, arrangements of bright-faced, exotically colored zin-

117

nias brought life to the room. At once the warden's encumbrance of tension began to slacken to simple fatigue.

Changing into old slacks, soft slippers, and his favorite baggy sweatshirt (the front of which said in bright blue letters, "World's Greatest Granddad"), he mixed a tall drink of Irish whiskey and water, settled from official-in-charge to man-in-repose on the terrycloth-covered lounge on the deck, and surrendered to the tranquilizing seascape.

Warden Tolson was a big man. Now in his late fifties, his thick, wavy hair was gray; his skin showed some brown spots and wrinkles of aging, but there was only a trifling sag in the powerful, athletically defined muscles, for he was generally diligent about exercise. His size and handsome, friendly face contributed to a self-confident, optimistic bearing free of conceit. He was a pragmatic man, gregarious rather than philosophical, one of whose talents was an ability to size up prison situations and make prompt, wise decisions.

His genuine interest in people and their lives, together with a remarkable memory for names and faces, made him popular among the 700 or so members of his staff. As he met them on his frequent unceremonious rounds, subordinates at every level were quietly delighted by his ready, first-name greetings. How gratifying to be remembered by the man in charge! His lively sense of humor and hearty laughter as he asked about their work, a daughter's graduation, or a recent jaunt to Las Vegas invited confidence and informality. It was not his nature to direct and control his staff by means of wrathful criticism or intimidation nor was such a heavy hand often necessary, for very few would wish to suffer the ignominy of failing their hero's respect.

It was not unusual for him to visit the cellblocks or to walk the precipitous, wall-top catwalks from one lonely guardpost to another in the middle of the night, spending a few moments in ordinary conversation with isolated watchmen.

"Hello, Charlie. How ya makin' out up here in your penthouse?"

"Evenin', warden. I'm doin' fine, sir," the officer would respond, both pleased and shy with his visitor.

"Kind of cold in here—what're you doin', savin' money on the gas bill?" the warden laughed.

"Naw, I don't pay no attention to the gas bill. Gotta keep it cool in here else I might fall asleep."

At the same time, it was clearly understood that the warden was inflexibly serious in his expectation of conscientious individual performance for the fulfillment of the institutional purpose, which was, as he often explained, "to protect society by securely holding the people they send to us, to keep them from tearing each other–and ourselves–apart while they're in here, and to send them out when they've served their time as better risks than they were when they arrived. That's a big order, but it's our only reason for being here." His was the ultimate, pervasive conscience of the place: brutality was unswervingly forbidden, and his devotion to justice was never corroded by vengeance.

Quite humanly, the warden's subordinates, most of whose sense of purpose and capabilities were more modest than his, centered their main concerns and ambitions on their personal lives, their own sets of joys, challenges, and sorrows, content to follow his leadership and draw from his strength for the job. They seldom stopped to consider the immensity of his responsibilities, simply taking for granted that he was competent to properly and tirelessly manage any prison situation that might arise.

For their parts, many of the 5,000 inmates categorically detested the warden for his role as The Man, their firm keeper, but the thinking ones gave him at least grudging respect for his absolute fairness and for his calm reasonability, which had defused some tough situations.

On the occasion of one uncommon prison task, however, the people around the warden had come to recognize, albeit with some surprise, that even he had moments of considerable personal strain. The task had the substance of a serious drama played out over an extended number of sleepless hours; it was of such profound legal, moral, and emotional consequence that it was necessarily closely overseen and, at critical points personally directed, by the warden himself. Over the years it had come to be a common in-house understanding that even when the drama's climax had been meticulously achieved, its audience had dispersed, and all related details were officially documented, its finish awaited one last, informal, very private act of the warden.

This was the public side of the man who now lay watching with vague attention as the orange and deepening-red display of the sunset changed into stars and darkness. Finishing a second drink, he withdrew from the cooling night air to the shelter of the room, where he kindled the fireplace and adjusted a background of music.

He was not an obsessive person; he did not dwell moodily or self-indulgently on the weight of wardenship or the special strains of the past few hours. Rather, he settled into a restorative acceptance of his present surroundings–the isolation, the fire, and the music. Taking his time, he went to the kitchen, heated a bowl of clam chowder, ate it with pleasure, and, when he had had enough, turned to cleaning up the slight disruption of the workspace, deriving satisfaction from performing simple, basic tasks. Perfunctorily, he moved back to the living room window and stared out at the night sky. Catching sight of the lights of a coastal freighter far out on the ocean darkness, he watched it move slowly northward like the phosphorescent tip of a great minute hand reaching up from deep below, tracing the earth's circumference.

Becoming drowsy, he stirred the fire, banked oak logs on the embers, poured a brandy nightcap, and stretched out heavily on the vast, comfortable Hawaiian lounge.

Twenty-two hours ago, more or less, as was his custom on the night before a scheduled execution, the warden had visited the man held in the cheerless cell of the ground-level gas chamber annex, which poked out midway along the east side of the prison's massive wall. Aside from the bleak surroundings, no two such meetings in that location were ever the same, varying with the nature of the capital crime and the personality of the condemned. Last night's visit was unique not only for the qualities of the inmate, but because the warden and this inmate had met in the death cell "for the last time" more than once over a period of several years.

The condemned was a man with an inexhaustible will to live, a drive well-served by his exceptional intellectual gifts, which, through remunerative publications and various legal maneuvers, had kept him on death row for many, many months of due process delay beyond the date originally ordered for his execution. During that time he had, in fact, been moved here to the grim steel vestibule of death on five taxingly suspenseful occasions, only to be temporarily reprieved by a last-minute call from a district judge, the governor, or the United States Supreme Court.

Incidental to their conflicting official interests, a conditional rapport had developed between the two men, the inmate always denying his guilt, fighting for his freedom, and the warden fulfilling the assignment of society to hold onto him and carry out the court-ordered sentence. Each knew exactly where the other stood. However misshapen and detestable the man's felonies, his unyielding determination to stay alive and his talent for devising/inventing/creating the means of doing so were impressive, if tiring. "What such abilities, otherwise directed, could have accomplished for mankind!" the warden often thought. And the condemned had come to see the warden as an uncommon man, unswervingly firm, eminently fair and humane within the limits permitted him by the public whose servant he was.

Stepping into the cell, the warden spoke in a congenial, matter-of-fact tone. "Good evening, Lyle."

His face flushing slightly, the convicted man rose from the bunk where he had been writing with pencil and paper. He smilingly responded, "Evening, Warden Tolson. Here we are again!" His manner was that of a maitre d', formally pleasant, controlled, coolly welcoming a powerful patron, but screened behind the charm one sensed an anomalous, shifting presence. Inappropriate, somehow, to the setting and the circumstances, he presumed a too hale-fellow familiarity: "Taken any bets on this time, warden?"

Looking down, the warden chuckled softly, crossed his arms over his barrel chest with some embarrassment, and answered, "No, I only bet in poker games."

"Here's an inside tip: I'll be back in my regular cell on the row tomorrow night. You can bet on it! My lawyer's got a new point, workin' on a reprieve from the governor. It'll be in by morning. I expect to be cleared and out of here within the year!"

At the close of the brief visit, a meeting without acrimony or sentimentality, and one in which the condemned man made no special last-minute requests, confessions, or statements of remorse, the warden departed the annex. Entering the prison proper, he walked directly to the captain's office, the nighttime nerve center of the prison, to confer once more regarding the temper of the institution in the hours before the scheduled execution of its most notorious resident.

No scientific poll had ever been taken, but it had often been observed that, although ordinary inmates despised the nature of the condemned man's crimes, they were bitterly jealous of his ability to beat the death rap for as long as he had. At the same time they hated the state for its determination to get its terminal pound of flesh. It was a smoldering ambivalence requiring custodial caution.

With friendly seriousness, the warden eased into a chair across from the captain at his desk.

"Evening, captain. You look like you've got things well in hand. What's going on in the cellblocks tonight?"

The captain responded that throughout the prison, total if sullen calm prevailed. "If anything, it's quieter tonight than usual, but all of our officers are staying alert."

The warden was satisfied that no major security problems were likely to erupt within the walls. After a few moments of small talk, he said goodnight and walked across the yard, saying to the sally port officer who let him out, "Have a good watch tonight, Henry," and headed on up the hill past the administration building to his own quarters.

The one other possible source of trouble and a major unknown factor of the night lay just outside of the prison gates, where, on the public roadway leading up to the perimeter gate, a gathering of several hundred people were maintaining a protest against capital punishment. For hours the group had been there, orderly and compliant, in no way defiant of the unobtrusive but constant surveillance of the state police, who sat in their vehicles at strategic viewpoints some distance from the crowd. Should the gathering grow more demonstrative or violent, its control would not fall on the warden or his staff, but would be the responsibility of the police or, if necessary, the militia.

Still, word of the protestors' presence was carried within the walls by the ubiquitous prison grapevine and had an elusive effect; any disturbance "out there" could increase the tensions inside, a potential to which staff must not overreact, but for which they must be prepared. From his bedroom window, the warden could see that many of the crowd's members had settled for the night on the floodlit flat beyond the gate, some stretched out in sleeping bags while others sat up around small fires. If all went well their demonstration would remain passive throughout the coming critical hours.

In accordance with a jury's finding, a judge's sentence, and after all of the years of minute legal review, the execution had finally taken place. To the resting warden that now seemed long, long ago, but it had been earlier today, yes, just this very morning before his drive out here.

An execution is not a funeral. There are no prayers, no music, no gun salutes, no eulogizing declamations. An execution is a process, next beyond the plucking of an eye, the pulling of a tooth . . .

The official witnesses, the condemned's attorney (who was the only woman present), the official doctor, the reporters–some swaggering and blase, others sensitive and subdued–had entered and taken seats with the warden in the minuscule, sickly green ampitheatre.

In front of them, at a few moments before ten o'clock, the condemned man, with the poise of an actor on a tiny stage, was escorted by four uniformed officers from the holding cell to the small, windowed, heavy-steel cubicle in the cramped room's center, where he submitted to the emplacement of straps binding him to the solid metal chair. He held almost ostentatiously still as two of them rigged the stethoscope by means of which the doctor would listen to his heart and announce fulfillment of the sentence. As the officers stepped self-consciously from the chamber, closing and dogging the airtight door, the man's eyes met those of his pale, stressed attorney for a moment; then he sat motionless, awaiting the sure-bet call of reprieve.

On this day no interrupting call came from any of the powerful state or federal officials to whom last-minute appeals had been directed. The red wall telephone at the warden's right shoulder hung silent. The only sounds were of the breathing, an occasional cough, and the scraping feet of the onlookers.

When the hands of the large, black-rimmed electric clock on the wall crept to an instant past 10:00 a.m., the warden, taking one glance at the inmate—almost as if to affirm that he was still there—soberly nodded, briefly closing his eyelids, signalling an official somewhere out of sight of the onlookers to effect the mechanical drop of the cyanide pellets into a waiting container of reactive solution. The killing fumes rose up quickly.

The condemned's defiant smile and deliberate deep breathing were his only benediction.

By noon all of the formal steps of the killing process had been completed. The clutch of elbowing reporters had rushed off to file their stories, variously describing the fulfillment of a six-year-long course of justice. The deceased's few personal things—a typewriter, law books, letters—had been signed over to his attorney by a subordinate official. The custodially vital midday count, scrupulously maintained in the captain's office, had been reduced by one. A waiting hearse rolled from the secure outer doors of the death annex along the narrow blacktop between the granite wall on the left and, to the right, the waters of the bay on whose muddy edge six red flamingos stood one-legged, dozing in the warm sunshine. The ironically luxurious conveyance stopped at the gates for inspection against surreptitious passengers—stranger escapes had been pulled off—then moved past the straggle of remaining protesters and merged with the freeway traffic.

Only one unannounced, unofficial custom of the terminal routine awaited enactment: mid-afternoon, as somewhat curiously expected, the warden departed the institution grounds, leaving the prison, its duties and personnel behind.

The sun was up with the promise of another glorious day when the big man awakened from a deep and, for him, prolonged sleep. The smell of fresh coffee roused him fully, and he felt warmly grateful for the thoughtfulness that it meant: Mrs. Escalante had been there, noiseless in the kitchen, had started the brew and returned to the caretaker's cottage. More than did so many who took his strengths for granted, this tiny woman and her husband recognized the man's ability to bear a warden's burden, but touchingly, they also knew that this did not exempt him from the pleasure—even the occasional need—of some kindness for himself. "What friends, what friends they are!" the warden spoke aloud.

Rising, he felt wonderfully refreshed. Thoughts of the previous day's work had been slept from his mind. Looking out at the bright sunshine, he quickly decided to delay having a cup of coffee until he had first taken a jaunt along the winding trail to the beach. "I'll stretch the muscles, pump up the old heart, clean out the lungs, and then come back for a shower and have a bite to eat!"

It was early afternoon when the warden's car was seen returning to the penitentiary. Vigilantly signaled by the gatehouse officer, a muscular trusty inmate in carefully pressed prison denims swung open the cyclone-wire gate and, flourishing a smile, called out, "Afternoon, warden!"

"Afternoon, Sam," the warden called back as he waved a greeting to the officer in the shelter beyond.

Dialing the warden's secretary, the gatehouse officer reported, "Lucy, the warden's back. He's just driven in."

In turn, the secretary phoned the warden's principal deputies and the captain, saying simply, "The warden is back."

Invariably, the responses were the same: "Oh, good! And thanks for calling."

Just how many executions there had been in the warden's twelve-year tenure Lucy did not recall—it was a good number—but she knew, as did the others, that the routine was not finished, that the prison and its personnel were not "back to normal" until the warden had been to his beachhouse overnight.